VETERAN FLIPPER

A Real Estate Investor's Flags

to Riches Journey

Chris Bedgood

1st Edition

Disclaimer

---◆---

I have many proud veterans of many wars in my family tree. So I humbly dedicate this book to our nation's Veterans.If it wasn't for your sacrifice and selfless service, we would not be able to live in a free society that allows us to believe in our American dreams, nor would we have the ability to work hard to make them a reality. Thank you for giving us the Freedom to choose our own destiny!

---◆---

Table of Contents

What's Your Flags to Riches Journey?

———◆———

"Flags to Riches" is obviously a play on the phrase "Rags to Riches." To me rags to riches means to take massive action and change the way you make money and the amount of money you make, quickly and purposefully, with definitive results that then allow you to change your life for the better. Let me repeat the important parts of that statement: *Take MASSIVE ACTION and CHANGE the way you make money and the AMOUNT of money you make, QUICKLY and PURPOSEFULLY.* And if you have taken the time to pick up this book and read that sentence, then you have already begun your rags to riches journey. Don't stop now!

Finding your own rags to riches journey is my goal for you, and that's why I wanted to write this book. It's exactly what I did in my own life and how I built my own successful real estate investing business. I went from having a boss and a J.O.B. to being my own boss, in charge of my own destiny. There are a lot of books out there that will tell you the steps to take to become a successful real estate investor, so why should you read this one? What makes my version different than any of the others? Let me start by saying one thing. I encourage you to read my book *and* everyone else's, especially if you are a budding real estate investor. The more you can learn in this business, the more successful you'll be.

This book is packed with:

⇒ Tips others often forget to include, especially on how to find deals.

⇒ Strategies that will let you earn while you learn.

⇒ Tactics to create the ultimate safety net so you earn more with less risk.

⇒ Behind-the-scenes looks at both *Flipping San Diego* and real estate investing.

My take on writing a book about real estate investing is not to convince you that this is the end all, be all book. In fact, I hope that it's a springboard to the next level for you. This book is written for the newbie, the seasoned, *and especially* the returning investor. Who is the returning investor? The one that has grown their business and income temporarily, had big wins but even bigger losses, yet has not given up hope and is ready to give it a go again, this time for good.

This book is about my own rags to riches journey. It's about trying to find a way to make more money and get past the per hour, salary + benefits, J.O.B. mindset that so many people have. When you think like that, you're making someone else's dream a reality, not your own. Let me repeat that because it really needs to sink in: *WHEN YOU WORK FOR SOMEONE ELSE PER HOUR OR FOR A SALARY, YOU ARE MAKING SOMEONE ELSE'S DREAM A REALITY, NOT YOUR OWN!*

Mine is a genuine story about someone who has set different goals throughout his life and has tried (successfully) to create his own luck and take advantage of the opportunities when luck presented itself; when opportunities became available. You have to create your own luck and take advantage of what's put in front of you, rather than not being able to take advantage of them and before you know it, they're gone.

I grew up in a middle-class family, in a fairly blue-collar neighborhood in the suburbs of Atlanta, Georgia in an average-sized suburban city called Morrow. My parents both did what they could to further their education and provide for their family, receiving their college degrees later in life, as parents of two rambunctious boys. I think that's where I get my love for learning and my drive to keep bettering myself. In fact, I am still learning and trying to educate myself more and more every day. You don't have to come from money to be successful in the business of real estate investing. You don't need a college education. You don't even need to know "the right" people to succeed. You just have to be willing to set your goals high, strive for success daily, and work harder than the next guy. I'm living proof of that.

Flags to Riches: Changing Your Mindset

"Once I changed my mindset, there was no stopping me."

In order to achieve your own riches, you have to change your mindset, which is something I'll talk about often and in more detail throughout this book. I have been changing my mindset since I was a young kid. Many circumstances helped drive me. When I was a teenager and my parents got a divorce, I grew up a lot and quickly. When I was in the Navy, I went through a lot of difficult times. I learned about the importance of accountability: keeping myself accountable and keeping others accountable. Those were some hard lessons, but they helped shape the person I am today. I'll tell you more of my story in a little bit.

While enlisted in the Navy, I was often much younger than those around me. I was working hard and being promoted quickly. I remember an incident very clearly that was a true shift in my mindset. At one point during my service, I had been promoted two pay grades higher than my best friend; I was now his supervisor. One day, he tested me by defying me. I had to make a decision – am I going to be a leader or a friend? I knew that if I did not report him to my superiors and let him be insubordinate, I would have been seen as a false leader and lose the respect of those I was in charge of. If I did report him, I ran the risk of losing a friend. I made the difficult decision to write him up and report him. I reminded myself that I had a job to do. It wasn't my fault that he wasn't being promoted as quickly as I was, and I had to make the decisions that I knew were right, no matter how difficult.

It's the decisions you make, especially the difficult ones, which will propel you forward and shape your life or push you backward and disrupt your life. Either way, the choice is in your hands. What choices will YOU make? This book is a story about taking advantage of opportunities. I still take advantage of opportunities every chance I get, and I am by no means done. I'm making my own luck every day (**Bedgoodism #3: Make Your Own Luck**).

Bedgoodism? What's a Bedgoodism?
Sit tight, I'll get to that in a little bit.
But believe me, you'll want to pay attention to them!

Having a show on TV (the wildly popular *Flipping San Diego* on A&E and FYI Channel) is not the end of my journey; it's just a part of my journey. I'm moving forward; I have more stories to write, some I don't even know about yet. In this book, I'm going to take you through the stages of becoming a successful real estate investor – from getting started as a birddog, then shifting to wholesaling, then moving into rehabbing and flipping, and from there, who knows? You will only be limited by your motivation and drive. I'll share my experiences and things that worked for me, things that I'm still doing today that are working better than ever. I'll talk about some marketing strategies you can use, show you how to build your network, how to find AND how to fund your deals using other people's money (O.P.M.), and perhaps most importantly, strategies for finding buyers and sellers. I'm also going to share some specific, real-life case studies of deals I have done including how we got the houses that were featured on the show, *Flipping San Diego*, and a few examples of wholesale deals that were not used in the show (but I think are really good!).

Bedgoodisms for Success in Life & Business

———————•◆•———————

"I've lived my life and some of yours, too." - Chris Bedgood

Before we focus on the nitty gritty of building your real estate investing business and getting you on the road to riches, I think it's important to share some of the philosophies that I live by. I call them **"Bedgoodisms."**

What's a **Bedgoodism**, you ask? You've already seen me mention a Bedgoodism, so let me talk about them for a minute. Bedgoodisms drive who I am. I've coined a lot of them, and others are interpretations of what I've learned from other motivated, driven people throughout my life. They are present every day of my life and guide how I deal with other people, my business, and my passions. They have been in my life almost as long as I can remember and I hope by sharing them, you'll want to incorporate at least some of them into your life as you strive to take control of your own destiny. I consider **Bedgoodisms** part of my character, but I use the term very tongue-in-cheek. They're not *rules* for you. I'm not suggesting that if you don't follow them, you won't succeed. No, of course not.

My reason for sharing them is to get you to think about what drives **YOU**, and how you can use those philosophies to shape your business and your life. I've experienced a lot of the things that you'll go through as a new investor, so take my advice to heart and see what a difference it can make for you. Here are my **Bedgoodisms**, briefly explained. You'll see how they factor in to my life and business throughout the book.

1. **Don't Be Afraid To Fail... Forward** – Taking five steps back and one step forward is not a bad thing, it's just *another* thing to keep you moving. If you keep pressing ahead and focusing on your goals, before you know it there will be a shift to five steps forward and only one step backward. It's an amazing feeling once this happens. Failing is *normal* and part of the deal.

   You may have seen this equation before, but it's a super important part of this Bedgoodism:

   Don't be afraid to fail. Instead, be afraid of not learning from your failures. Now start failing... forward!

2. **Motivation: Create Your Own Destiny** – No matter what, keep growing, living outside your comfort zone, and doing, meaning, "make stuff happen **EVERY** day." Set your

goals and take hold of your own future. Don't let someone else design it for you.

3. **Make Your Own Luck** – Create your own opportunities and choices. Choices are great, but if you're only trained to do one thing, you've limited your choices. Look ahead and find out what others have done to get there; then do just a little bit more. Establish goals and set yourself up for that next step. Success is not a lottery ticket that you buy. I don't believe luck has anything to do with success. "Luck" is about *maybes*. It is about leaving your own destiny in someone else's hands. Why wait for luck? I think it is instead about creating opportunities. I don't buy lottery tickets because I don't want to collect tickets. Does that make sense? I only really want the *winning* ticket! So **I create winning transactions. Winning relationships**. I make my own "luck." There is no such thing as luck once you change your mindset and realize **luck is just an opportunity that came your way that allowed you to do something that someone else can't or won't do**. Don't WAIT for luck. Instead CREATE luck (opportunities) by getting ready for it to present itself so that you can turn the opportunity (luck) into MONEY.

4. **The Law Of Exponentiality** – Make things happen and before you know it, more great things will begin to happen from the momentum. Two things become four, four becomes eight, and so on. Never give up, and always surround yourself with successful, like-minded people.

5. **Networking & Face Time** – Real estate investing is a relationship business. The more people you can meet and

bring into your network, the more options you have. Networking and face time is about creating bonds and connecting with people. Tell everyone what you're doing, surround yourself with like-minded people, and with successful people. Learn from them and establish a good follow-up system. Get rid of everything negative that clutters your motivation or any nay-sayers. Sometimes you have to completely clean out the closet (yes, this can mean friends, family, J.O.B.s, lifestyle) to move into your next phase of success. Cleaning out the closet and starting fresh is incredibly powerful and motivating. Start TODAY!

6. **Measure Your R.O.T.: Return On Time** – Everyone knows about R.O.I. (Return On Investment), but what about R.O.T.? For every hour of time you invest, what are you getting in return? Time management will be crucial as you're building your investing business. Don't let wasted R.O.T. let your ideas and goals R.I.P. (Rest In Peace). How much per hour are YOU worth? $50? $100? $1,000? $10,000? Shoot for the moon. Manage your time. Money is not a sign of success in my mind; my Return On Time is!

7. **Treat Your Daily Life Like A Business** – "Do what others don't do now so you can do what others can't do later." You've probably heard variations of this saying throughout your life, and it's true. Set goals for yourself, establish accountability, and start to think and see things differently. **The key here is to hold YOURSELF accountable because nobody else will!**

8. **Perfection Can Be Your Enemy** – Throw perfection out the window and you'll have a better chance at succeeding; you just have to get stuff done and make it happen. Perfection-Perschmection! Once I gave up on trying to figure out every little last detail and started throwing stuff up against the wall to see what would stick, I learned faster and succeeded exponentially. Quit being a perfectionist. You aren't building the space shuttle; you're just trying to build your income.

9. **Know Your Risk Tolerance** – As an investor, you need to know your risk tolerance and what's at stake. If you're just starting out, find a mentor, someone to bounce questions or situations off of. It will make your ability to go under, over, and through barriers *much* easier and faster. Work with your mentor to determine your risk tolerance. The higher the stakes, the more is at risk. The higher the risk, the more money you can make, but maybe **not**. Risk tolerance is different for every level of investor. *KNOW YOUR LEVEL.* Get your feet wet first so you don't drown on your first deal. Let somebody else take the risk. Wholesale to someone with more risk tolerance than you. Cash a fat check and keep swimming along for another day. Turning down risky deals *is* investing; it's part of the business.

10. **Finding The Right Mentors** – Having a good mentor is essential when you're getting started in real estate investing. A mentor can guide you through the process, help analyze a lead or deal, help determine your exit strategy, and help find funding (or be the source of your funding). I can't emphasize this Bedgoodism enough. Mentors will save you

R.O.T. and R.O.I. They will keep you from drowning (R.I.P.) and the expense, or splits, or investment, or whatever deal you make with them for their very valuable time will pay you back over and over and over and over. Mentors will increase your speed to success in unimaginable ways. Don't skimp. Even if you have no money, find a way (I will teach you some techniques in this book). Get a mentor. Today.

11. **Being A Pessimistic Optimist Can Be A Good Thing** – Definition of a pessimist: *A person who habitually sees or ANTICIPATES the worst.* Definition of an optimist: *A person with the disposition or tendency to look on the more favorable side of events or conditions and to EXPECT the most favorable outcome.* The point of this is: looking at deals through rose-colored glasses is not necessarily a good thing for a real estate investor. You have to ANTICIPATE eventualities and prepare for when things go wrong. This doesn't mean to be negative; it just means to be cautious. Remember, there's a lot at stake in a deal, so don't get caught blindsided. Do everything you can to prepare for any eventuality. Just like an aircraft mechanic might. I think being a pessimistic optimist is the definition of being a good aircraft mechanic. You, as the mechanic, are always anticipating why this airplane "might" fall out of the sky and doing things that will prevent that from occurring before it "might" happen. But you must be an optimist too, because as humans, we aren't supposed to fly. So the mechanic and the crew are super optimistic that all the flight systems will work or they would never get into an airplane. When investing or flipping houses, the same rings true. When you buy the house, you must assume the

worst so that you don't have too many surprises. This is a pessimistic attitude. But at the same time, you *must* be an optimist because you are expecting to make a profit, right? Being a complete optimist in real estate will get you in trouble fast! Cool your jets. Take a step back. Make sure your investor hat is on tight, and then go for it!

12. **Hold Yourself Accountable, No One Else Will** – No one else will be as invested in your success as you. There will be doubters every step of the way – don't be surprised if they're your own family and friends. Remove any excuses from your life. Remove as many negative wall-blockers as you can, and set up your own system to hold yourself accountable to your goals. Figure out how to make things happen. One of the techniques I used early on and still use today, is to post large, 8 ½" x 11" notes all around my house... on the bathroom mirror, refrigerator, TV, in my car, at the office. These motivational notes remind me that I am my own success formula, and that at the end of the day, nobody cares as much about my success as I do. Not even if you have a spouse or business partner. Partners can come and go. Partners should and can help keep you accountable, yes. But at the end of the day, it is you who is in control of your own destiny, nobody else.

13. **Learn To Say No** – "Yes" isn't always the best answer in real estate investing. Understand the power of no, especially as a negotiation tactic that can be used with other investors, real estate brokers, contractors, and on and on. A "yes" can end up costing you a lot of money. This ties in closely with knowing your own risk tolerance.

14. **Find People Who Believe In You… And Leave The Others Behind** – Believe and invest in yourself before you invest in others. Find someone who believes in you and it can be life changing because it will allow you to move forward. You will move to the next level in your growth as a person and as an investor. Real estate is a people-driven industry, especially when you are first starting out. You will need people who believe you are a performer – the "real deal." Find those people. Leave all the others behind immediately.

15. **Learn The "Take Away"** – Leave people wanting more. Make yourself valuable. Then make yourself *invaluable* and people won't know what to do without you. This is a skill that must be learned. One minute you're attainable, but then all of a sudden you're not. Just walk away or get off the phone first, or don't reply to an offer on your flip house for a whole day. Learn the "take-away" and it could change your results instantly.

16. **Find A Way Around The Wall… Any Way** – There will be obstacles in your path to your goals. It's your job to find a way around those obstacles, any way you can. If a wall is put up in front of you, go around it. Go under it. Go over it. Find a way to climb it. If it's blocked, go back and find another way. Just figure out how to get past it. Be willing to do things that other people or investors won't do and that will set you apart. Have a "no excuses, never give up" attitude and no wall will ever defeat you!

BONUS: **Sharing The Wealth Has Made Me Wealthy** – Treat the people you work with well, and don't be afraid to share the wealth. Doing this will motivate the other people to continue to perform and prove their value to the situation. Help the people around you build their riches and it will build your own riches even faster!

Chris Bedgood: The Real Investor behind *Flipping San Diego*

———————◆———————

From the U.S. Navy – To Licensed FAA Aviation Mechanic – To Real Estate Investor – To Infinity & Beyond!

I'm a proud 3rd generation military veteran and veteran of a foreign war – my father (Navy – Vietnam) and both my grandfathers (one Navy – WWII, one Army – WWII) were in the military. I served in the United States Navy for seven years, and during the Gulf War Operation Desert Storm. Being a Navy veteran is part of who I am, but it's not all I am. Being in the Navy taught me a lot of lessons that I still carry with me today and helped shape my mindset.

I want to give you a look into my background so you can further understand how I got to where I am today and how my life lessons helped shape and define my journey. I've faced a lot of difficult things in my life and went through some rough patches, but I keep pushing forward, carving out the life I was meant to live. I'm going to be very transparent because I've had a lot of things that I've had to deal with in my life, just like you might. But, I always found a way to get past any obstacles that were blocking my path (**Bedgoodism #16: Find A Way Around The Wall... Any Way**).

As I mentioned earlier, I came from an average, middle class family. My parents worked hard to provide for my younger brother and me. But as a teenager, my world began to shift. When I was about 15½, my mom asked my dad for a divorce. She was a beautiful, intelligent, and strong woman who wanted to live life. She had dated my father since they were in high school. In her 30's now, she started to feel like life was passing her by, and she wanted something more than raising teenage boys, working hard as a nurse, and taking care of a family day in and day out. I don't blame her, and it took me years to understand how she felt. One night, after telling my brother and me that she was going to divorce my father, she shockingly and suddenly swallowed a whole bottle of pills and started to pass out, but my dad was quick, realized what was happening, and saved her. He scooped her up and drove her to the hospital to have her stomach pumped. Fortunately she survived. It was a frightening evening; one that I will never forget. It was at that moment in my life that my mind seemed to wake up. I was suddenly more mature than I could have imagined. From then on I became very independent and self-confident. I was on my own.

It seems like forever ago now, but a year or so after that, my mom moved out of our home to go her own way, so at that time I made a decision to go mine. When I was only 16, I raised my right hand at the local recruiter's office and committed to joining the U.S. Navy and serving my country. I knew I wasn't going to get into college with my abysmal grades, and I didn't want to stay around Atlanta working at Dairy Queen, so following in my Dad's footsteps seemed like a great idea, get paid to "see the world" mentality! But the Navy wouldn't let me head off to boot camp yet because I was too young and still needed to finish high school. Finally when I turned 17, during my senior year of high school, my dad signed for me and I enlisted in the Navy. I enjoyed my last summer as a civilian and prepared to go to boot camp on Sept. 2, 1987. I was ready to get out of town; I am an adventurer at heart. I wanted to be in aviation; I wanted to be a helicopter pilot. But when I actually was getting started in the Navy, the only position available was a Hull Technician or HT rating, which was a welder in the bottom ships. Ugh.

I knew that was not right for me, so I talked to my recruiters every day before heading off to boot camp to see if an aviation job had come available. Every day was the same story: *"No, but call back tomorrow."* So on the last day at MEPS (Military Entrance Processing Station), before getting on the bus to boot camp I asked ONE MORE TIME. After talking to the final MEPS recruiter at the last hour, the recruiter did a final search and surprisingly informed me that a job came up for an Aviation Electrician's Mate or AE rating, and was I interested in that? Hellooooo! Heck yeah, Mr. Recruiter dude, I mean, SIR! I was super excited and didn't realize at the time how this one final question to the recruiter and one moment in time would change my life forever. I tell this story because it points to my drive at a young age. I never give up. I will ask, not beg. I am always going to see what I can do to get what I want. And the rest is history since you are reading this book right now.

My first year in the navy was in trade schools: Aircraft electrician school, then Naval Aircrewman school, then in-flight mechanic/Flight Engineer training. Finally I received orders to be stationed in Sigonella, Sicily, Italy, and I was again very excited. From ages 18 to 21, my job was to fly passengers and cargo all over Europe, the Middle East, and North Africa. I also participated in Operation Desert Shield and Desert Storm. I was having a great time and living life to the fullest. I continued to rise quickly through the ranks in the Navy and by age 21, I attained the rank of E-5 (a 2nd Class Petty Officer, which is basically a Sergeant in the Army or Marine Corps). After seven years in the Navy, it was time to get out and end my Naval career. I was only 24½ years old when I was honorably discharged. The Navy was good for me and good to me. I learned a lot of valuable lessons, including how to respect people and how to be held accountable and held to a higher standard. Prior to enlisting, I had a tough time dealing with authority figures because I had a lot of angst growing up. The Navy helped me deal with that.

Before I got out of the Navy I was trying to decide, *"Who am I? What do I want to do with the rest of my life or at least the next five years?"* I knew I wanted something more; I didn't want to go backwards. So, I analyzed my options and started to figure out what that "something more" was (**Bedgoodism #2: Motivation: Create Your Own Destiny**). During my last year in the Navy while stationed at NAF Washington, D.C on Andrews Air Force Base in Maryland, I decided I wanted to get my FAA Airframe and Powerplant, or A&P license, so I could continue working on airplanes and doing what I loved, but as a civilian. It was then that I had my first crack at networking. I worked with civilian aircraft mechanics while still enlisted. I talked with them, I asked questions, and I listened. Plus, I did the dirty jobs that they didn't want to do, and I gave them respect and in the end, earned theirs. I was happy. I was working on planes, learning everything about them from how to fix them and keep them from falling out of the sky to how to wash them. I did whatever I was asked to do and was willing to get my hands dirty.

Because of the relationship I was able to develop with these mechanics, when a position suddenly opened up out of the blue, I was offered a job to fill that spot before I was even discharged. I would be earning $14 per hour, working in the exact aircraft hangar I worked at while I was enlisted. Woo hoo! One day I showed up for work in my Navy uniform, and literally the next day I was working as a civilian and growing a beard. (My squadron had two aircraft types; one was worked on by the military and one by civilian contractors.)

After nine months in Washington D.C. as a civilian, I got a call from management about an offer to go to our company's satellite operation in Sicily, working at the same airbase I worked at while I was in the Navy. How exciting! I still had friends there. My company said if I took this position, they would send me anywhere I wanted to go afterwards. It was a win-win situation and a no-brainer. Going back to Sicily as a civilian instead of being constrained by the rigidity of the military? I'm in! Plus, I always wanted to go to Southern California, so in exchange for my going to Sicily, they ultimately created a position for me in Orange County, California at a satellite operation our company had there.

Why am I telling you this story? You have to create your own luck like I did by working with the civilian mechanics while I was still on active duty just so if a position opened up in the future, I might be at the top of their list, and that position did open up! Set yourself up for success so that when an opportunity presents itself, you are ready to take it (**Bedgoodism #3: Make Your Own Luck**)! After my civilian stint in Sicily, I moved to Orange County, California, the land of sun and fun. My life was amazing. While I was working in Southern California, I learned that one of my favorite aircraft manufacturers had an assembly plant nearby. It was the pinnacle of private jet aviation, Gulfstream Aerospace. Yes, I wanted to work on Gulfstream jets! I had experience working on them in the Navy and they have a manufacturing plant in Long Beach, so I applied for a job there. Why not leave the great, cushy job I already had so that I could go to a more stressful and tougher job, right? I wasn't satisfied. I always wanted to get better and do bigger things. Gulfstream was that next step. Or was it? No luck. They didn't have a position for me. Hmm, no position doesn't mean NO to someone like me. It doesn't mean they don't "want me." It only motivated me. I just had to keep calling so that when a position came up or if the company grew, I would be fresh on their minds.

My strategy worked! (**Bedgoodism #1: Failure + Persistence = Success**) I kept applying and networking with their mechanics and management until someone gave me a chance. The hiring manager rode a Harley Davidson motorcycle and so did I, so I made sure I went on rides that he went on. *Do whatever it takes to get to know the people who can influence your income or life.* One day a position became available, and guess who they called to interview for it? Now, getting a job at Gulfstream was no cakewalk. It was a highly sought-after place to work. Once you got in, you realized that working for Gulfstream was a hard job; they wanted the crème of the crop working for them and they expected results. I seemed to be on the edge of being fired many times, but my supervisors knew I was a hard worker who could listen and could be trained. That was something I learned in the Navy. They believed in me, which was motivational. **Bedgoodism #14: Find People Who Believe In You... And Leave The Others Behind.** Keep charging forward.

At Gulfstream, I was working with people who were older than me most of the time. I was only 25 years old when I started there, but I worked hard and learned as many skills and technologies as I could so that I would be invaluable to the company. I was "creating value" in myself. So when I was being promoted, it was because I was the best candidate for the position. I made sure I learned all the systems; I wanted to be the guy in charge. But I still wasn't satisfied. My goal was to be something even bigger. I wanted to be the guy in charge of a private jet. I wanted to be a private mechanic and work for the people who actually owned and flew these $25 million jets. When the planes would come into the Gulfstream service center for maintenance so would their crews. I networked with the private mechanics and with the owners of the planes every chance I got. I kept in contact with them. I let them know I was available. I followed up. I created my own luck. Follow-up is key in any business, especially real estate investing. *People, including bosses, want to work with someone they know and trust. Networking is key to building trust and rapport in any business (especially in real estate).*

[The picture above is of me in Japan around 2002. I was hired as the private mechanic and flight engineer on this $35 million GV (G-Five).]

One day, one of the owners approached me and said he needed a mechanic and was willing to pay a salary of $40,000 per year. I was only making $18 per hour at the time and working as much overtime as I could, putting in 60+ hours per week. Earning $40,000 per year was a guaranteed salary and that sounded great. But wait, why would I accept their first offer without countering? *Everything is a negotiation. Always ask. What do you have to lose, right?* I took a chance and asked for $65,000, and he said YES! I was hired and worked directly under the head mechanic. Through working on the airplane I also got to know the owner of the plane better. I knew he was doing well because here he was with a $20 to $30 million airplane filled with skis, camping gear, and other things like that; he was basically using it as a Winnebago to carry around his toys. I told myself I needed to investigate how he made his money. One day I asked him, "How did you create your wealth?" His simple reply? "Real estate." His family had started working on houses, buying and fixing them up, and then got into developing from the ground up, from huge condo complexes to massive tract home subdivisions. That got me thinking. I was only working 40 to 50 hours a month, the rest of the time the owner was gone because he liked to fly. Since I had extra time on my hands, I was looking for something to do besides going to the gym and wasting time. I had the opportunity to do more with my time, even though I was tied to my cellphone in case something happened with the plane. If the plane broke down, I was expected to fix it either remotely via phone consultation or actually fly to wherever the plane was at and fix it on site. That limited my flexibility but not my drive and my motivation to do "more."

It was about this time that I received something in the mail about a real estate seminar, and since I was becoming more and more interested in pursuing real estate, I went to the seminar. I also started going to local REIA (Real Estate Investor Association) club meetings. I jumped right in. I found mentors. I joined coaching programs. I began buying properties and making offers on pre-construction homes. I was doing real estate deals on the side while working at my full-time job as a private jet mechanic.

During this time I began working for a different jet owner as his private mechanic; I worked for that owner until they sold their airplane. The new owners who bought the plane wanted me to come with the deal as their mechanic, which made me happy because I wanted to stay with Gulfstream jets and I knew this particular one inside and out. They asked, *"What do you want? What will it take for you to come over to our company?"* I was willing to take whatever they offered, but I figured I would throw something out there. Again, why not? I said I wanted six-figures. The owner of the company paused, then looked at his vice president, and said, *"Make it happen."* He wanted the security of knowing he had his own mechanic with his plane – someone who already knew it inside and out. The point of this story is to get you to remember to keep moving forward and always negotiate. (*When you negotiate, start higher than you are willing to accept. This gives you room to negotiate downward and make the other negotiator feel like they got a deal. It creates a win-win!*)

I learned a lot from these situations and have used these confidence-building scenarios to negotiate in my real estate business as well as in life. And it's made me a lot of money! But back to my budding real estate investing business. During the robo-signing days of 2004 to 2007 when banks would give you a loan if you could prove you could breathe, I got into trouble. I took out a lot of conventional loans and bought properties "wrong." Every bank on the planet was willing to lend me money for some reason, and for some reason I thought this was a GOOD thing. Use debt as leverage, right? Well yes, and... *NO.* The economy and my speculative buying habits led me to crash and burn. I'm getting a little ahead of myself here, but I had nine properties go to short sale or foreclosure from 2008 to 2010. I know I'm not alone; I'm sure that many of you reading this book have gone through the same thing if you were doing speculative investing in the mid-2000s. I'm here to tell you, don't give up! Get back in the game. Learn from your mistakes, and you will be stronger than ever, just like I am.

Don't Be Afraid to Get Out of Your Comfort Zone

Let me quickly tell you a story about a time in my life where I made another big change and got out of my comfort zone and made a risky move that turned out to be worth the risk. In 2007, while working as a private jet mechanic for the company that had offered me the six-figure salary, I got into a disagreement with the new chief pilot that was hired after I was. The pilot felt one way about an issue and I felt the opposite way. But at the end of the day, the chief pilot was my immediate boss and I had to do what he said even though the owner of the company was the one who actually hired me. I had to have the plane ready for a "pop-up" flight that had been scheduled. I expressed that "Yes, the airplane is safe to fly," but I felt it needed more time in maintenance for troubleshooting intermittent glitches that were hard to duplicate on the ground, when it was not in flight. But while I was ordering parts and trying to get more maintenance performed, it became clear that this very wealthy company was seemingly not able to pay their bills. For a mechanic this is a nightmare scenario because it means I might not be able to get vital parts to repair the airplane before the next flight. There was pressure on me to save money on maintenance but still have the plane ready for flight. But I was not allowed to talk to the owner about the bills; he seemed oblivious to the issue. There was a situation where the airplane had a glitch on a flight overseas. In this particular case, the glitch caused the flight to be delayed at its next stop while we performed troubleshooting over the phone. After the plane returned from that trip, the owner was told that the glitch was my fault and that the delay was also my fault. I was the fall guy and was unceremoniously released from my position a few days later. Holy cow. I was making $100,000 per year and now I was making ZERO. My peers at other companies were making much less than I did, even if I could find another job (which was doubtful because there aren't many private mechanic jobs out there). I got a little scared, to say the least. I have to admit that by this time, my mind was already on real estate. Getting released was almost a relief. I was escorted out of the building; given no notice and no severance pay. A meeting of the minds was not happening. That was ok with me because I was already changing my mindset. I had flipped the switch in my mind.

I was still good friends with the Director of Maintenance at the first company I worked for many years before, and the next day he offered me a job for $80,000 to come back and work for him! My initial thought was, "Woo hoo, I'm saved." But WAIT! Hold 'yer horses fella! That was a lot of money, BUT I had a decision to make. Here's where my life changed *AGAIN*! I could either go with what was safe and take the job, go back to my comfortable life, or *not* take the job, get WAY outside my comfort zone, and go full-on into real estate and maybe one day *own my own plane*! I asked my long-time friend to give me two weeks to make a decision, and I would then let him know. During those two weeks, I decided to attend more REIA meetings. This was where the action was and where other investors would be. I needed to jump into making a decision: do I take a cushy job or go after real estate riches?

I was living in Costa Mesa, California at the time, but while attending a REIA meeting in San Diego, one of the scheduled guest speakers was an established, well-known, and respected investor. My girlfriend at the time lived in San Diego and said I "must" go see this investor speak. So of course, I went. He gave a great presentation and said he was still investing and always would. He said part of investing is also selling. Something I was *not* doing. I was only buying. What caught my attention next was when he said, *"If you own something now, you need to sell it because the market is crashing."* This was May 2007. Huh? Crashing? No way. I was still buying property, but this guy was advising me to *sell*. What?!? I owned seven or so properties at the time. I felt like an "equity millionaire," an armchair investor, living the good life, buying, speculating. This was an "OMG" moment for me. I think I realized, deep down in my gut and like a ton of bricks hitting my chest, that I had been "investing" wrong. I had been following what the herd was doing but not paying close attention to what the cycles were doing. This one REIA meeting changed my life. And that is why I encourage every new or seasoned investor to attend REIA meetings, mastermind meetings and seminars several times a year, if not several times a *month*. It may just save your bank account. You can check out the one I went to at www.SanDiegoREIA.com. I was too late. What I learned saved one of my properties, but not the others.

I had some decisions to make in my life. I was just let go from my six-figure salaried job, and I was just told that all my real estate was going down the tube and on top of that, I needed to make a decision on whether or not to take a new job making $80,000 per year or go full time into real estate with no income whatsoever. Great. Why not just jump off a cliff? **Bedgoodism #1: Don't Be Afraid To Fail... Forward.**

San Diego-Bound

I always wanted to live in San Diego, so I decided to sell my primary residence in Costa Mesa along with just about everything I had and move to San Diego. *I turned down the $80,000/ year job.* I knew I could get part-time work as an aircraft mechanic for $50 an hour if I needed to, plus I had credit cards I could live off of. No risk, no reward. Small moves equal small results. I made a bold move and undercut the market to unload my house. It was great timing because within two months the entire housing market changed and the major banking institutions began to fail (August 2007) and house values began to plummet. Most of the nation was still in denial, not believing that big banks could fail or that real estate could *decrease* in value. I moved in with my then-girlfriend and started my real estate career. Things did not go well for two years. I did what I had to do to survive. My girlfriend didn't think I was going anywhere and it started to show quickly in our relationship. I was struggling. Eventually the relationship fell apart. I was motivated to not depend on her or anyone else, so I moved out, got a cheap apartment, and took contract aircraft mechanic work with my friend in Long Beach to make ends meet and pay for rent, gas, and the Ramen noodles I was eating. I couldn't even afford a beer with friends, so I stayed in and worked.

I commuted from San Diego to Long Beach, sometimes working five days straight, 20 to 30 hours at $50 per hour, sleeping on the office floor or in my car. During my off time or on breaks I would hit the phone and emails again. I was taking calls, working deals, and faking it 'til I made it, every day, like a freight train with nowhere else to go but forward.

*Note: The takeaway from this section is, if you or someone you love is thinking of a career change or leaving their job to go into real estate, there is a way. But **you** have to make it happen. Write down what it will take to live and stay healthy and work in real estate. Get rid of everything else, and sometimes that means getting rid of your boss! The key is planning. I am not encouraging you to fire your boss until you are ready financially, physically, and mentally.*

My friend repeatedly offered me that full-time job, but I turned him down. I knew this was my chance to follow my dream. Going back into aviation full time was not part of that dream, and that turned out to be my main motivation. Just as I had this realization, the aviation company I really enjoyed working for (before the six-figure company) called and wanted me back. They had a new plane that was based in San Diego, and they wanted to offer me a job for $60,000/year. My dream, now, was to be in real estate. But I was struggling financially and this was instant money to get me back on my feet *and* it was in my new hometown, San Diego. I knew that I could do this part time and have money in my pocket, but I would be at their beck and call. I asked myself, *"What will it take to make me happy?"* What would it take to get me back into my comfort zone instead of out of it? I decided to negotiate high. So I countered at $85,000 + benefits knowing they most likely wouldn't go for it, but kind of hoping they would. They turned my deal down, and that was ok. What was meant to be was meant to be. Or not, in this case. I was scared. I had turned down a secure job that would be there for me for many, many years.

But when I really analyzed it, I decided I only had one chance to break free and follow my dreams fully and completely. Go big or go home. I went big with my counter offer. They told me to go home.

Real estate investing of any type was difficult for me from 2007 to 2009. The country was trying to figure out if we were going into a recession or possibly another depression, and every cable news pundit had something negative to spin about the economy and real estate. That's when I stopped watching the news. Negative news wouldn't get me anywhere. Real estate is based on cycles, not cable news. Banks seemed to be closing their doors and being rescued by the government daily. I couldn't sell my investment properties. They were all upside down; they were worth less than what I owed on them. Banks didn't even have short sale departments back then and when they did, they weren't organized enough to get a short sale done before a house went to foreclosure. So I lost all my properties to some type of foreclosure or take-back. This was devastating and embarrassing to me. I stopped telling people I was a real estate investor. I went into a moderate state of depression. It was difficult to get out of bed. Difficult to socialize. Difficult to push forward. But I couldn't accept that; it seemed like an excuse to me, and I don't live my life around excuses. If an airplane falls out of the sky, it's done. It's over. No excuse will bring it back.

I woke up one day with that mentality – that I couldn't let myself fall out of the sky. I needed to get my wings back and figure this out. After some deep self-analysis (and a few self-help books), I decided to see a doctor to help me with my depression. During the diagnosis, I took some tests and discovered that I had a form of Adult A.D.D. (Attention Deficit Disorder). It turns out I've had it since I was a teenager, and it had affected me both negatively *and* positively throughout my life without me knowing. A.D.D. can cause severe frustration, even anxiety. It can be difficult to socialize or finish tasks, all of which can lead someone with A.D.D. into depression, clinical or otherwise. But I also found out A.D.D. is very prevalent in people with high IQs, especially entrepreneurs. Once I discovered this about myself, I felt a sense of relief. I now knew why I was the way I was, and it would allow me to recognize when it was a problem or when I could use it in a positive way.

"You can troubleshoot anything in your life, whether it's an airplane or your brain."

For full transparency, along with eating better and regular exercise, I take a mild prescription medicine to this day to help me focus and deal with my A.D.D. I tell this story because I think it's important for entrepreneurs to not let anything get in your way. Find out what is holding you back and fix it or adjust to it so that you can keep pushing forward Mack truck style, no excuses style.

Time to Make a Big Change... Again.

So rather than give up, I decided to use the skills and talents I already had. I would become a real estate agent. Ugh. (No offense to the thousands of hard-working agents and brokers out there, but my goal was to be an *investor*.) At least this way I would be surrounded by real estate, and I might even be able to make a commission every once in a while. But I didn't want to work in an office and drive buyers around. That seemed time consuming and frustrating. Instead I tried brokering pre-construction properties in Arizona, West Virginia, and Georgia. I was the middleman. I would find investors and then pass them off to the developers and hope they would close and I would receive a commission. I failed. I tried selling to Canadians. I heard they had money and loved buying in the States. That failed. I then tried brokering pre-construction properties in Costa Rica to Americans for three months. I even flew people down to Costa Rica, but the deteriorating economies of America and Latin America caused that venture to fail.   I was kicking myself for not taking the $60,000 aviation job. Kicking myself, but not running backward. It was a pause of self-doubt, but in my heart I knew I ultimately made the right decision. Once you flip the switch, you are locked in.

By now I had pretty much given up on investing. I was a little jaded, and my risk tolerance was way down. Plus my credit was shot, and I had no money. I once again changed my way of thinking. I needed to stay close to home and concentrate on my local market. There was plenty going on here in San Diego. So my new goal was to be the #1 real estate agent in San Diego County. Really? Yes, really.

"San Diego's on sale... come on in!"

I went to work for a real estate broker in downtown San Diego where I practically lived on the "up desk," which is where real estate agents take incoming calls and wait for pedestrians to walk in the door. I had gotten my real estate license many years earlier, but I really had no experience as a bona fide real estate agent. This broker gave me an opportunity. She interviewed me and even with my lack of experience, she could see my drive and wanted to take a chance on me. She was another person who believed in me along my journey, and it was a turning point in my life. This broker's office had a lot of street traffic, and I would talk with everyone who passed by. It was here where I cut my teeth on being a salesperson and learned how to sell, how to speak the lingo of real estate, and how to bond with people. I was somehow able to do what people said was impossible, sell people on buying high rise condos when the market was terrible. I bonded with people; I would make a connection. I was doing one deal every couple of months. I survived mainly on my credit cards and small commission checks. But I wasn't working on airplanes anymore! I was moving forward. Kind of...

Besides working as a real estate agent, I was still constantly networking with investors and going to REIA meetings. I was already working with an established investor, trying to find him bulk REOs (properties owned by banks that they would sell off in bulk packages or "tapes"). In a way it was like "chasing unicorns," The banks were failing and no one knew anything for certain, but there was always a daisy chain of people and brokers who swore they knew the bank asset manager and could get you the properties for a small commission or point. But the properties never materialized. A lot of time was wasted, but the up side is that I began to form a bond with another investor.

By December 2008, I was burned out. I decided to leave town for a few weeks. I used some left over airline miles, and I went to Thailand and Cambodia to go backpacking and clear my mind. I even attended the famous Full Moon Party and went to the ruins of Angkor Wat. I almost didn't come back, and there were many days I wish I wouldn't have. I ultimately decided to return from Thailand because my new investor friend and I were in the final stages of sealing a bulk REO deal, which could have made me a $50,000 finder's fee. I flew back to the U.S. on New Year's Day 2009 just to close out this deal. At the very last minute, the investor didn't like the deal and turned it down. I realized then that my life was too wrapped up in other people and their financial decisions; my own finances and success were too wrapped up in other people's decisions. I was frustrated and again felt up against an insurmountable wall. I was disappointed that the deal fell through, but I was learning that this was part of real estate. Many deals fall through. I didn't break off my relationship with the investor, but I did quit trying to find bulk deals and instead again focused on being a great real estate agent. I was back from the beautiful, lush beaches of Thailand and regretting it every day.

But since I was back, I needed to regroup and get to work. I thought to myself, "Who sells the most REOs around here, all over San Diego, not just downtown?" Through some of my networking I had met the president of the San Diego Association of Realtors. He was a first class Realtor/broker with his own company. He was the number one selling broker in his franchise, and he had hundreds of listings. This is the place I need to be, fully in the mix, not working for boutique offices. I need to go big or go home. So I met with him and said I wanted to work for him. I had very little experience, but I had a massive work ethic and wanted to make him money and work for his company. He agreed and got me an interview with the vice president, and I was off and running.

I began working the up desk, taking calls. I did open houses on other people's listings. I door knocked. I did mailers. I was driving buyers all around town; I was desperate to make deals. So desperate that I can remember one difficult buyer who was the type who thought everything in the world was wrong; she had many phobias. Plus, she had a massive Great Dane who was actually qualified as a service dog and traveled with her at *all times*. This was not going to be easy, but her parents needed to do a 1031 Exchange and decided to use the money to buy a house for their daughter, which I knew would mean instant money for me. All I had to do was find her a place to live. (A 1031 Exchange means a seller can sell an investment property and exchange those funds into another investment property and avoid paying capital gains *if* done within a short amount of time. If a new property is not found quickly, then capital gains have to be paid, which can cause lots of tax problems. So people doing 1031 Exchanges are generally in a hurry and are willing to close quickly. It's money in the bank for the broker, and that's what I needed. But, oh boy, was I in for a frustrating time. Who said being in business for yourself was easy?) I fired her three times. Yes, I fired my client! I had to drive her and her Great Dane everywhere to look for the right house. No one else would work with her. I was driving my 3-series convertible BMW, so each time we went looking at property I would have to put the top down in order to load the giant "service dog" into the back seat, then put the top back up. It was a hilarious sight to see in downtown San Diego! After many weeks and many migraines, I eventually found her a new construction condo downtown, got her in, closed the deal, and I made a $10,000 commission. I learned a big lesson just then. Take the low hanging fruit, no matter how frustrating, and get paid. Keep plugging away. Sometimes it will mean taking five steps back but one big step forward.

I was slowly becoming a successful real estate agent and I was ready to do more. I still was not thinking of investing yet. I was going to REIAs all over San Diego County and going to seminars. I was networking (always as a real estate agent), doing everything I could do. I even tried brokering commercial real estate. In the fall of 2009, I received a postcard "teaser" to go to a guru's real estate investing boot camp. I decided to go so I could meet other investors and network. There I met an investor who was flipping houses in San Diego County. He happened to be a retired Navy pilot, so we instantly hit it off. I drove him around town, and he pointed out how much he made on deals as we drove by those houses. It made me cra-zy! He was flipping and making money in *this economy?* No way. Hmm… I've got to re-think this. I still did not have an investor mindset. I was the one driving the investors around. I was the real estate agent. I had taken my investor hat off and permanently replaced it with an agent's hat.

Until that day…

Making the Change

It was then that a switch went off in my head. "Why am I trying to be the 'best' real estate BROKER I could be?" I changed
my mindset, and from that moment, I knew that I wanted to
be the best real estate **INVESTOR** I could be. I wanted to be
in control of my own destiny. I wanted someone driving **ME**
around (**Bedgoodism #2: Motivation: Create Your Own Destiny**). By now it was 2010 and I knew I had to team up with
an established investor in order to learn as much as I could. I
began calling people that I already knew. One of the investors
I had met on several occasions agreed that if I found a deal, I
could bring it to him, and he would work the numbers. This
investor happened to be someone I had worked with in the
past, and things didn't work out so well back then. *But*, because I didn't burn the bridge, I was able to contact him and
get my investment career underway again. In real estate investing, it's a small world and can actually be very cutthroat.
Things move quickly. There is so much money to be made
that you have to watch what you do. You have to keep your
leads close and set expectations early. When you're just starting out, don't be surprised when things fall apart. Just do everything you can to prepare, which will be much easier with
the guidance of a strong mentor. I started to strategize with
this investor. I was making calls off of signs. I called Realtors;
called about dumpy, dilapidated houses. I always represented myself as someone who could perform (as an *investor*, not
a real estate agent). I'd say things like, "*I need to buy five houses
a month. I already have two, but I need three more. Can you help
me?*" I did this even when I didn't have any houses yet. Fake

it 'til you make it. I just needed to get the deals in the right hands, and to do that I needed to prospect for deals. Dig, dig, dig. Do what others weren't willing to do. Dig one more foot. Turn over one more rock. Make one more phone call. Knock on one more door.

Soon after, my investor friend started turning down deals that I thought were good and I wasn't sure why, but it made me realize I was too tied to one investor, so I began finding other ways to close the deals by seeking out other investors who had different investing criteria. My motivation was that I would strive for more, knowing I would end up with more knowledge, more contacts, and in turn more success. I haven't looked back. I still, today, will partner with other trusted investors on deals, but I'm not tied to someone else's business model or criteria. I have my own network, my own contacts, my own strategies, and my own tactics. Most importantly, I have my own goals. Even though I've paid my dues in the investing business, I am still learning and growing every day. Each deal brings me closer to my goals, which allows me to strive for new ones.

"My Name Is Chris Bedgood, and I'm a Flip Addict"

I love doing what I do. I love to be on site, watching the guys work, making design decisions, making changes, and creating someone's next dream house. However, I don't like to do a lot of the actual work because it takes me away from scaling or growing my core business, which is buying and selling houses. That doesn't mean I won't get in there and get dirty when I need to, but I need to make sure stuff gets done. I prefer to leave the actual rehab work to the experts (contractors whom I trust). I like to be the one running the show behind the scenes. There's a lot of time, energy, and hard work that goes with real estate investing, especially if you're a new investor and *are* your own company. But it's addicting. It's fun, and to me, there are a lot of rewards:

⇒ **You get to learn about yourself.**

⇒ **You can make great money.**

⇒ **You get to design great houses and show them off.**

⇒ **You get to be in charge (which I love).**

⇒ **You get to help people in desperate situations.**

⇒ **You get to beautify neighborhoods.**

⇒ **You save homes, credit, and sanity.**

⇒ **You create safe living environments for renters and/ or first time home buyers.**

⇒ **You help people own a home again.**

⇒ **You create dream homes!**

It involves a lot of work and a lot of time, but I wouldn't trade it for anything. It's so exciting when you get paid, and that reward should grow bigger with each deal you do.

Why Real Estate Investing?

———————•◆•———————

"Real estate investing is not a get-rich-quick business, but it can change your life quickly."

The opportunities and possibilities in real estate investing are virtually endless. You can completely control your own destiny. You may hear gurus or other experts claim that you can make $50,000 in 30 days by following a simple system. Yes, that can happen and it does, but don't automatically expect it to. It takes persistence and hard work, plenty of let downs and failures, and doing what others won't do. In real estate investing, you have the potential to make extremely large profits on just one deal (I'll show you a couple of those examples later). Or, if you're not ready to dive in completely, you can make some extra money to supplement your salary, virtually while you're driving around town or to and from work.

Real estate investing has allowed me to live the lifestyle that I've always wanted to live. It's made things that used to be just out of reach, attainable. Things that I used to really have to think about I can now do without a second thought. I've had some good years, some not so good years, a couple of *really* not so good years, and some great years (especially the past couple). I'm living my bucket list now. I'm not waiting until I'm retired to do the things I've always dreamed about doing. Since beginning real estate investing, what's changed for me?

⇒ I have a wandering spirit and have traveled to 30+ countries. (I secretly wanted to be a travel book writer, and that attitude is still what keeps me motivated to be successful as a real estate investor.) I've backpacked around Thailand and Cambodia, Costa Rica and Panama, Europe, parts of Australia, and parts of the Middle East, just to name a few. I go on cruises and road trips around the U.S. whenever I can. I force myself to leave the business I have built and just get away. My advice? Find a friend in another country and make an excuse to go and visit them. You don't need to stay with them, just touch base when you get there and before you leave, and then go make your own adventure.

⇒ I'm on my third Harley Davidson (the one you see in the *Flipping San Diego* opening) and have my eye on my next one. I've ridden over 45,000 miles on my Harleys, including riding from Long Beach, CA to the world-famous Sturgis Motorcycle Rally in South Dakota. I love the Harley spirit and participate in things like *The Love Ride,* an annual motorcycle event to benefit MDA – the largest one-day motorcycle fundraising event in the world. To me it means being free.

⇒ I used to not be able to afford to go to concerts or entertainment events, especially at the last minute. Now I don't even blink. I just buy a ticket, and the ticket I want. Rock concerts, the circus, boat races, Globe Trotters, super cross. Sometimes I buy four tickets and take friends without asking them to pay me back – to me it's networking.

⇒ I can go to Las Vegas whenever I want. I don't gamble,

but I love the energy, the hotels, the restaurants, and just hanging out.

⇒ I am able to hire a personal trainer and receive private attention rather than having to go to a gym.

⇒ I can go out for sushi dinners, not just on half-price night!

⇒ I'm a bargain shopper and always will be, but now I can afford to buy any online group coupons that catch my eye, even the exotic ones (houseboat rental on Lake Powell, driving a NASCAR race car, trips to exotic locations, flying a jetpack, etc.), and I still feel like I'm getting a deal!

⇒ I've attended a party at the Playboy Mansion (every man's secret bucket list item).

⇒ I bought an RV. I not only use it for road trips, but I'm a bit of a "prepper," so in case of a disaster, mass electrical outage, volcanic eruption, tidal wave, or the impending zombie attack, I can load up my family and head to safety in complete comfort.

⇒ I am living out dreams I had as a kid. I always wanted to learn how to play the guitar, and I'm doing that now with private lessons!

⇒ I can afford to buy "toys" like a huge, flat screen TV or new computer, without selling my soul to the credit card company. Cash is king, and no debt feels good.

As I realized success in my real estate investing business, I noticed that my mindset began to change. I noticed I wasn't as stressed as I used to be. You will find that your whole way of thinking will change; you're not worried about buying the cheapest toothpaste or the bargain shampoo anymore. Trust me, I'm a bargain shopper, but the difference now is when I want something extra, I don't have to stop and think about it. I'm disciplined (I'll explain more about that later), but I have more options now. Little things you want are now attainable, and this can grow exponentially if you're careful (**Bedgoodism #4: The Law Of Exponentiality**). Start slow, take your time, and keep working it, **BUT YOU HAVE TO START**! Don't be afraid of failure because from failure comes learning, and each time you learn, you're taking a step forward. It's **Bedgoodism #1: Don't Be Afraid To Fail... Forward**.

After taking five steps backwards and one step forward enough times, soon you'll be taking five steps forward and only one step backward.

The Stages of a Successful Real Estate Investor

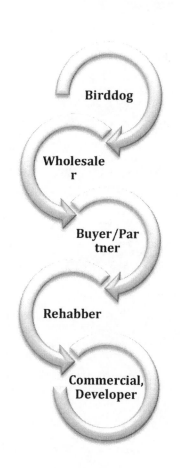

When you start your journey to become a successful real estate investor, you'll go through several stages:

This represents the natural life cycle of a successful real estate investor and includes a likely evolution of learning, success, and growth. There's one more important thing to know about this progression. **As you move through the stages, you're also increasing your level of risk** – your financial risk and the amount of time involved in each deal. Keep that in mind as I walk you through each stage and gauge it against your own level of risk tolerance. This brings me to **Bedgoodism #9: Know Your Risk Tolerance.** Risk tolerance will be different for every investor.

If you're a new investor, your risk tolerance needs to be low; you can't tolerate as much risk because you can't tolerate an empty bank account. If you're a more experienced investor, you will be better equipped to get around any barriers that come up and figure out what level of risk you're willing to assume. If you're wholesaling, you'll want to have a big list of investors because each investor will have that different risk tolerance level, some are willing to risk more than others, some are willing to risk less. Their business model often drives it, whether they are profit-driven or volume-driven. Having a range will help ensure that no matter what type of deal you run across, you'll have an investor that will be interested in taking it on.

This all circles back to mentoring and coaching – finding the right mentor is crucial to your success and growth. A mentor can help gauge your risk tolerance level and weigh all factors. If you're serious about this business, what you invest to get the proper mentoring and coaching will more than make up for itself, and it will help with the pitfalls that may come up.

A mentor can tell you when to walk away, sell to them, or to another investor on their buyer's list.

If you ignore the risk factor warning bells, you could be setting yourself up for significant problems down the line, jeopardizing the likelihood of successfully reaching your goals. And trust me, if you sour on your first deal, your chances of doing a second deal are slim. Real estate investing is about finding solutions, no matter what stage of the cycle you're in. You're providing solutions to other investors, to homeowners, or even to real estate agents.

Note: In this book I'm focusing mainly on the early stages of investing, specifically birddogging and wholesaling. We'll talk about moving beyond into partnering and rehabbing, but I want to make sure you're first locking down the fundamentals before you're ready to step up your game. Let's look at what happens at each stage of the life cycle.

Birddogging

The easiest and fastest way to jump into the world of real estate investing is to start out as a birddog or someone who seeks out deals and passes them off to other investors for a fee. As a birddog, your job is to identify potential deals for other real estate investors. It's that simple. Think of yourself as an apprentice investor.

Why the term birddog? Well, you're not going out into the field to track down houses that have been shot out of the sky! What you are doing is searching for properties; you're hunting for gems, for money, to bring back to the hunter, the investor. As a birddog, you're not risking any of your own money; you don't have to quit your full-time job. You're usually not tying up a property. You don't need to have access to the MLS or to an investor-friendly real estate agent (we'll talk more about what that means later). If you do have those things it will help, but you don't have to have them to be a successful birddog.

What you do need is motivation, the ability to shift your thinking, and the willingness to invest your time. In exchange, you'll be able to earn anywhere from $500 to $1,000 or more for each lead you turn over to an investor that converts to a deal, just for having a keen eye. The amount you can make or negotiate is really up to *you*! As a birddog, you'll need to start looking at houses differently than you do now. You'll want to look for signs of neglect – peeling paint, missing shutters, neglected landscaping, piles of old newspapers, broken windows. If you see these indicators, make note of the address and pass it along to an investor, who will take it from there.

You can even take it a step farther and do a little research on your county website to find out who the owner is and share that information, too. When you find out who the owner is, you can use online services such as spokeo.com to locate and learn more information about the owner. But really, that's it. You'll also want to open your ears when you're talking with other people. Listen for certain trigger words that may indicate that they have a house they would be interested in selling, things like divorce, death of a loved one, foreclosure, being "underwater," or probate. Those can all be signs that they want to take action, and can mean money in your pocket. When that happens, start a conversation to learn more about their plans for the house and then explain how you would be able to help.

Everyone thinks that real estate is about property. But really *it's about people*. Relationships with people. People who have money. People who have problems but who have property. All kinds of people. Tune in. Listen up. As a birddog, your goal will be to create relationships. You don't need to know remodel costs; you don't need to know about contractors and permits. You are finding an address and phone number (ideally) and turning it over to an investor as a dry lead. You really don't need to know anything about the property beyond that. If you do, that's a bonus, but generally, the investor will take it from there.

Change your money mindset. When you're starting out, maybe part time, don't necessarily get caught up in the millionaire mindset which can seem daunting, but maybe rather think of the money you can earn as a new birddog as "Christmas bonus" money. Everybody with a salaried J.O.B. hopes for a Christmas bonus. Why shouldn't you get one? It's money you can use to buy Christmas presents or gifts for friends and family. It's not replacing your income, just supplementing it. As you gain knowledge and your network grows larger, you can adjust your goals and shoot for being a millionaire. If you have multiple investors, you can really boost your supplemental income stream. One of the decisions you'll have to make, once you gain experience and are bringing in more leads, is expanding your investor pool. However, if there is one investor who is turning into more of a mentor, you will want to consider remaining loyal by giving first right of refusal to him or her. If that person isn't quick enough to react or just doesn't have the funds or time, then it is "time" for you to shop the deal to another investor.

Note: In my business, once I get a deal under contract, I shop my deal to my favorite investor first. But I immediately set in motion my back-up plan and tease my top 10 investors that I have another deal, and I'm wondering if they are looking for another one. If I get one on the hook, then I let my favorite investor know that I would need an answer quickly, or I will have to move on to my next investor. You should do this too. To grow or scale your birddog business or any business, you need to have more than one option. Most professional or full-time investors know that if they don't look at your deal quickly, they may lose out to another investor. And none of them want that. That is why your birddog business can be a gold mine for you, and I can show you how to set that business up almost overnight.

As a birddog, change your mindset immediately. Start to look at houses differently as you're driving around town. Look for tall weeds and overgrown landscaping, peeling paint, fallen shutters, roofs with missing shingles, fences falling down, broken windows or boarded up doors. When you see those things, you're driving by money! It's about changing your mindset at this point. Ugly houses are going to be gold for you. As just an average resident you may see a house and think, *"It's ruining my neighborhood,"* but when you are trained to have your birddog hat on, you'll see it as a glorious opportunity to not only earn money, but also fix up the neighborhood.

Set aside one day on the weekend and start driving around. In the business of investing it's called *Driving for Dollars*. Bring a notepad and your camera or smartphone and take note of the addresses of the houses that you think are candidates. If you get in the habit of doing that regularly, you'll train your mind to look for these signs regularly (**Bedgoodism #7: Treat Your Daily Life Like A Business**). Put your birddog hat on and think, *"How can I get the information into the hands of someone who can do something with it?"* When you get home, do your research and find out whom the house belongs to. Check your county website and learn as much about the house or the owner as you can. Then, turn it over to your trusted investor and, hopefully, mentor as a potential lead.

You have to be persistent and do this regularly. You might not hit the jackpot on your first try. But you MIGHT! It will take lots of looking, but the payoff will be there once you start seeing checks come in to you. Eventually something will happen and when it does, doors will begin to open (**Bedgoodism #4:**

The Law Of Exponentiality), your confidence will grow, and success will begin to build. It's the law of averages. If you don't start looking, you'll never earn a fee. If you don't bring a lead to an investor, you'll never get a check. If you don't make the decision to change your mindset and look at houses differently, you'll never make it as a birddog, and you'll never achieve the riches you're looking for.

I started out as a birddog. I was working on airplanes part time to get by, but I was also working as a real estate agent and was surrounded by houses, buyers, and sellers. I was also attending REIA meetings and going to investing seminars and boot camps. I had no life, but I had a goal. I had drive. I got my priorities in line. I did what others weren't willing to do so that I could one day live like others can't. Financially independent! In control of my own destiny. As a birddog, you do not assume any risk; you do not have to perform. You're simply passing information along to an investor. The burden of closing the deal shifts to the wholesaler or the investor. They will work the numbers; they will write the check. It's your job to bring them the deal.

"A lead is not the same thing as a deal... not every lead will turn into a deal."

Keep in mind, you won't earn a birddog fee for every lead you turn over to an investor. Why? Because a lead is not a deal. You'll earn a fee for a lead that turns into an actual deal for that investor. If they get paid, you get paid. If they don't, you don't. So the quicker you learn what a lead looks like, the quicker you can reach your riches goals. A good mentor can help make the distinction clear for you.

From Birddog to Wholesaler

I said this earlier, but it bears repeating again. Everyone thinks that real estate is about property. But really *it's about people*. Relationships with people. People who have money. People who have problems, but who have property. All kinds of people. Your job as a wholesaler is to get to know the people and connect them together. Your reward is the fee you get from making the connections. Wholesaling is about flipping the contract, not the actual property. Wholesaling is a quicker payday than the more advanced stage of rehabbing, but you usually make less. Less risk, less reward. You're becoming your own boss at this point. You're proving your value to investors. Now when they get a text or email or phone call from you, they'll check it out faster and make running the numbers on your leads a priority. This is important to understand. Provide value and you will be rewarded.

As a wholesaler, you are once again looking at houses differently. When you identify a house that might make a good investment property, you'll need to have a general understanding of what it will take to rehab the house. Understand that you're not going to be doing the rehab work, but in order to know the After Repair Value (the ARV) of the house and what an investor can resell it for, you need to understand the general cost of what you think the numbers will be.

When you wholesale, you are actually tying up the property through a contract, unlike birddogging. You normally have a signed agreement with the seller (even if it is written on a napkin). That means no one else can take that property from you for x amount of time. You're building your reputation. Sometimes you're actually putting a deposit down on a property ($100 to $1,000 to tie it up, sometimes more so you can beat out the competition and show you are serious). You can now sell or trade your agreement with a seller or real estate agent to an investor for a negotiable fee. The stakes are higher because if you don't perform, your reputation can be damaged, and you might lose your deposit. **One word of caution:** The worst thing a wholesaler can do is get greedy. Again, take a quick reality check when you hear you can make a $100,000 wholesale fee, much less a $10,000 or even a $1,000 fee on every deal. Every deal is different and there may be a time where you get that $100,000 wholesale fee. But the more important thing is to understand the numbers, ask your mentor questions, and be realistic about the potential of a deal. Greed could equal no deal at all. The idea is build a business, not retire on your first deal, so figure out how to do the deal to where it accomplishes that. Not the reverse. A lot of gurus will try to convince you that real estate investing is a four-hour a week type of business. The reality is you have to work hard and stay motivated. The rewards can be slow or they can be quick, and once you've established yourself and gotten your systems down, it could be a four-hour a week business, but you need to start by getting that first deal under your belt. Learn to pick up on what people are saying when you talk with them (death, divorce, behind in payments). Don't get too caught up on the condition of the property. No matter the condition, there are investors who will work with it. When you're wholesaling, don't really shy away from anything. That's why it's important to have a big list of investors that you can contact, no matter the property. REIAs are your best source of investors.

It's a cool feeling when you can get a shabby, dumpy, neglected house under contract and make a pretty penny for yourself in a short amount of time! Be aware of one thing. As you become more skilled, you can quickly get a bad reputation with investors if you don't understand remodel costs (if the costs are too tight and there is no room for error it could mean the deal is "too thin," which leaves no room for profit and wasted time for your investor). Learn to ballpark the costs of a remodel before you take a deal. Your mentor can help you with this. You'll want to have a general scope of work that tells what needs to be done to the house through the course of the rehab. For example, if you can get a house under contract for $200,000, maybe it will need $30,000 in remodel costs and will be worth $300,000 once it is finished. That's great information for your investor.

As a wholesaler, you can still work deals that a rehabber may run away from because you're not always assuming the cost of the remodel like a rehabber or flipper is. If your investor database is large enough, you can simply pass it on to someone else who has a different exit strategy, because this house fits into their business model, like a buy and hold investor or someone who is volume-based rather than profit percentage-based. *Note*: Volume-based means someone buys lots of houses and sometimes is okay with breaking even because it's a numbers game for them. They will buy thinner deals from you to keep their volume goals in line. Profit-based investors are usually smaller investors who want to do fewer deals and only buy deals that make a certain amount of profit that fits their criteria. Learn each type of investor's criteria so you can have them on speed dial when a deal plops in your lap.

As a wholesaler, learn about all the different exit strategies. REIA meetings will expose you to many different investors with different exit strategies and business models. As you're networking more and building your list of investors, be sure to segment that list according to the types of investors they are. Some are looking for long-term property investments and will almost pay retail; others are looking to place their money, while others only buy wholesales. Learn about and get to know different types of investors; ask what they're looking for.

Case Study #1: Two Birds with One Stone: Birddogging While Walking Your Dog

This case study is all about timing and follow-up – two critical components to any successful real estate investing business. While it is mainly about wholesaling, it has a big birddogging element to it, which you'll now be able to easily pick out.

My business was growing, and I was at the point where I needed help, so I hired a transaction coordinator. She also happened to be a licensed real estate agent. I trained her to start recognizing houses that might come up for sale – told her what signs (literal and figurative) to look for. One day she was out walking her dog in her own neighborhood and she happened to see a real estate agent putting up a For Sale sign in front of side-by-side houses that were in bad shape. The neighborhood is a fantastic area, and houses there are easy to sell. Since I got her to change her mindset, she stopped and began talking with the agent, asking questions and beginning to bond with him. She found out the houses were not yet on the MLS but would be soon; he was just starting the process. He told her they were investor houses and needed a lot of work. They had code violations (lead-based paint, asbestos shingles).

"Code violations? Heck yeah! That means more opportunity for me as an investor and less competition. Bad smell in a house? Smells like money to me."

My assistant explained that she worked for an investor and continued to bond and ask questions – about the property and about the real estate agent. She explained how she could get an offer on the property, and he agreed to write the offer. She took his contact information and said she would follow up with him; this way, we control the situation. That's when I got her phone call. I was distracted with another project, but she knew to keep pressing forward. She had made an appointment to look at the property and after seeing it, thought we should write an offer. She also found out that we were the first investor to call on this property and since she had already established a bond with the agent, we had a foot in the door. He was willing to represent us.

She made the offer, and they countered (that's when things get exciting because it means you're in the game). We made an offer on both properties since the same person owned them. We stuck to the original offer. I didn't want to come higher and get myself in trouble because I knew I had to deal with the code violations, which would add to my costs. The seller accepted our counter because we wanted to buy both properties, the agent liked us, and they only wanted to deal with one buyer. I knew it would be a difficult property, and I had another deal in my lap. After we got our offer accepted, I asked for a discount – a $10,000 deduction – since one house had peeling lead paint and would also need asbestos remediation. They agreed. Just by asking a question, I made $10,000. (This is a **secret ninja move**: Always ASK, ask for a price reduction, closing credit, or better deal from a contractor. Negotiate. You never know what you'll get!)

My goal on this deal was to not use any of my own money. They wanted a non-refundable deposit of $25,000/house within three days. There was a weekend in there so I knew I had a little extra time. I decided to try and wholesale the houses and make a little bit of money right away. There are investors out there looking for all sorts of houses (which is why you need to build your networking list: **Bedgoodism #5: Networking & Face Time**) and I had a short window, so I posted the houses on my San Diego REIA Mastermind Facebook page with the caveat, "Only serious buyers contact me." I got a bite. I was careful to set the precedent up front – have the $25,000 deposit ready or I won't even meet with you. I needed to make sure the investor could perform, so I needed to see proof of funds.

I was making it up as I went, learning along the way, and making stuff happen!

The investor sent me his proof of funds that evening. I then explained that I wanted to see proof of funds that he could close on the deal – $515,000 for *each* property. I met the investor at the property (it was actually a team of investors). We talked out front. They started whispering among themselves, and I knew the game was on! I was asking $600,000 for each. I knew they would try to talk me down, but they were hungry to buy. They countered at $580,000. That was great, but being me, I had to counter (I *always* counter). "You said you'd do $600,000. Why are we even here? I have to make a call." I walked a ways down the sidewalk and pretended to place a phone call, complete with gestures of frustration. I "hung up" my call and stood there for another moment, knowing they were watching me. I walked back. "He won't go for $580,000. We came for $600,000, so we need to get closer to that number." This gave them the sign that I was willing to negotiate. "$585,000." "I just said $600,000, not $585,000." I was letting them feel like they won; I was sinking the hook. "Do you even have the funds? Look. We're here, I don't want to mess with this anymore. We'll do the deal if we go down to your bank right now and get a cashier's check." I let them put up the deposit.

I followed them to their bank, and they proceeded to get $69,000 in cashier's checks for a total of $138,000. I explained I would make a copy of the checks; they would keep them for 24 hours to firm up their decision to buy, but they would have to wire $25,000 each into escrow for the non-refundable deposit on the houses. They agreed. The next day I called to ask if the deal was still a go. If so, I would come and collect the checks. Since there was so much money involved, I did a handwritten contract and emailed it to them, showing the wholesale deposit and the escrow deposit. In the background, I was lining up other things in case they did cancel so I wasn't stuck.

The next day I walked into their office and they handed me the two cashier's checks for $69,000 each. I explained I would not deposit the checks until the 3-day due diligence was over, thereby creating a relationship with the investors – I was being tough, but was willing to work with them. Once the three days were up, they put up all the money and they did close, giving me my biggest wholesale profit ever.

Back to the houses, the seller's agent didn't want to double-end and only wanted to represent the seller. Since my assistant bonded with the agent and was a real estate agent herself, she wrote the offer and received the commission on the sale, all because she was taking her dog for a walk.

The total profit was $75,000 EACH house, plus the buyer's commission for my assistant, all in less than 30 days!

The moral of this story? Learn to recognize the signs of potential real estate investing deals. When you see a real estate agent putting a sign in a yard, you could be the first one to get the deal! Real estate is a fast moving, competitive business. Be FIRST! Then, don't get scared if you don't know what to do next. Ask your mentor (**Bedgoodism #10: Finding The Right Mentors**), or call someone who knows what to do. Be willing to split the deal or pay a fee, but don't let the house get away!

Case Study #2: My First Wholesale Deal

When I did my first wholesaling deal, I was actually working as a project manager on my first rehab project. I'll tell you that story a little later on. Since I was trying to build my own investing business, I put a small cardboard sign in the back window of my car – a simple 8"x11" sign that said, **"Cash 4 Houses,"** with my phone number.

One day I was at the rehab house, and the immediate next-door neighbor came to talk to me. He wanted to know what I was doing with the house. He also said that he saw the sign in my car that I pay cash for houses. That caught my attention, so I said, "Yes, do you know anyone who is looking to sell their house?" It turned out that his brother was getting a divorce, and, although he bought his house before he was married, he put his wife's name on the title, so he now had to liquidate the house and just wanted to get rid of it. I quickly said I would buy the house, the scenario was right for me as an investor.

Here's the catch. I didn't have any money, but I still represented myself as a cash buyer. I was projecting what I did to the neighbor, which gave him the confidence to talk to me about the situation. As it happened, the house was located directly behind the house I was rehabbing and had the exact same floor plan. I knew immediately that I wanted to make this house my very first wholesale deal. But, that involved changing my mindset and getting out of my comfort zone. I had set goals for myself and knew I could not learn unless I started doing.

I met the brother, he told me his story, and I agreed to write an offer on the house. I literally wrote it up on a piece of paper, including a due diligence period. I signed it and told him to give it to his attorney to approve and to get his wife's attorney to approve it, and then we would do a formal contract. By doing this, I was tying up the property. I wasn't trying to be perfect (remember **Bedgoodism #8: Perfection Can Be Your Enemy**?). I gave the homeowner $100 to make it a legal transaction, and he gave me a receipt. I was totally winging it at this point – I had never opened escrow on a piece of paper before.

From the moment I got the handwritten contract signed, I was letting investors know that I had a potential deal. Properties were selling fast in that area. My remodel was now in escrow so I already knew the resale price on this house and knew it would be easy to wholesale. I eventually connected with an investor who was building his business and wholesaled the house to him. I made a $14,000 wholesaling fee. From that I gave the seller's brother a $500 birddogging fee, and I had approximately $1,000 in miscellaneous transaction fees. My net in 30 days was $12,500. My payoff on the house I remodeled was $15,000, but it took 3 months.

This was a case where I had to decide: do I keep the house to rehab and resell it for x amount, which could take 3 to 4 months, or wholesale it and make x amount in 30 days or less? I chose to wholesale it and move on to my next deal. And move on I did… in that same block. There was another foreclosure across the street that I bought and flipped. So in one block, I managed to do two rehabs and one wholesale. I jokingly refer to that block as "Bedgood Estates!" What made this scenario such a success is I had a strong mentor (**Bedgoodism #10: Finding The Right Mentors**), I asked a lot of questions, I listened, and I learned. This wholesale took my business to the next level.

Both of these case studies are examples of wholesaling successes. For a new birddog or wholesaler, don't get caught up in feeling like you have to duplicate these extreme successes. I included these examples to motivate you and show you what is possible in this business. Focus on the fact that I did a deal and made money. *I went out of my comfort zone and did whatever I had to do to make the deal happen, including making it up as I went!* These examples *are* possible for a new wholesaler if you've changed your mindset, keeping your goals in mind.

Focus on what you can give and not necessarily on what you can get. Learn from everyone else, but *just make stuff happen*. Every day! You have to do the extra things that others won't do; you have to be someone who actually does something with the information that you discover. No one else is going to get you out of bed or force you to work late. It's up to you to create your destiny (**Bedgoodism #2: Motivation: Create Your Own Destiny**).

Being an Investor/Buyer/Partner

Once you are comfortable finding, locking up, and assigning the deals through wholesaling, you may start to consider "keeping" the properties for bigger profits by changing your exit strategy from assigning the contract to buy, fix, and flip or buy, fix, and hold. When you make this shift, you may first start out by being a partner on a deal. This is when you can turn to your mentor or to other full-time investors in your network. This may be a case where you bring a deal (on which you've already run the numbers and are confident it is a good deal) and offer a split of some sort on the profits. That's exactly what I did.

When I was starting out, I found a property that I knew was a good deal. I found a private money lender and explained the deal, but I didn't have anything more to bring to the table than the lead. So I got creative. I proposed an 80/20 split on the net profit, but to make this seem attractive to this busy investor, I had to add more value. I proposed that I project manage the rehab of the property, yet he would have final say on all decisions. Plus I would be the listing agent (real estate agent) once the house was remodeled so I would get the commission on the sale. It was a win-win proposition in my mind, and the investor agreed! I was off and running. Instead of waiting for an investor to give me a solution on flipping my own income, I looked for a solution; actually I created a solution. I thought outside the box, kicked over the wall and found a way to make the deal happen while flipping my income at the same time. I asked, and was able to make a solid case that the private money lender gladly accepted. **Bedgoodism #16: Find A Way Around The Wall... Any Way.**

When you reach this point in your birddogging/wholesaling/investing business, it is vital that you have a strong mentor who can help guide you and answer any questions you have. Mentors can help evaluate deals and also come up with alternatives if there are roadblocks in the way. Sometimes the mentor is your investor partner. These types of mentors are happy to mentor because they need you to be successful and they want to make money on the deal, PLUS they want you to bring MORE deals = win-win! At so many points in my investing business I have leaned on the expertise of a mentor. I really can't emphasize this point enough.

When you're getting started, get the deal under your belt to get to the next deal. If you're partnering with another investor, take a little and let the other investor get the majority of the profit. Really? Yes. It's about getting the first one done. It's starting. You're gaining the trust of the other investor. Don't necessarily ask for the big profit on the first deal. You don't have as much to bring to the table yet, so it's sort of a proving ground for you. That's exactly what I did on my first big deal. Later, with other investors I got creative and got my share of the profit, PLUS I charged a $10,000 management fee to oversee the rehab. There are many ways to build your dream real estate business. Partnering and/or project managing is one of many. Get creative, and always figure out ways to make a better R.O.T. (Return On Time)!

I'm not perfect. I can have a hard time getting along with other people; I have my own issues. BUT, I am the guy who decided to do just a little more. And that is a positive issue, I think. No matter what, people know they can depend on me, and that is worth gold in the world of real estate. I have no set formula that I follow. Every day I adjust and re-motivate. I know how important it is to surround myself with successful people. I know how important it is to portray yourself as someone who can bring something to the table – even if it's just your energy and your drive. Build your credibility as you build your deals. Do what you say you're going to do, and start to be known as a performer. Remember, as a new investor, there is less room for error, meaning if you are going to jump into flipping houses using other people's money, or your own, as a new investor be cautious.

Rehabbing/Flipping

When you make the transition from wholesaling to rehabbing or flipping, you have the potential to increase your profits significantly (hopefully), but you're also increasing your risk factor. Once you're comfortable finding, locking up, and assigning deals as a wholesaler, you may start to consider keeping or flipping the properties for yourself. Now you're changing your exit strategy to buying, fixing, and flipping or buying, fixing, and holding the property. Rehabbing is a more advanced real estate investing strategy with a lot of different facets and moving pieces. For right now, I'm not going to go into a lot of detail in this book on how to be a successful rehabber – I'll save that for another time. What I do want to do is explain the big picture of rehabbing and how it is the next step in the life cycle, and a natural progression for many (not all) wholesalers.

As a rehabber, you're ideally buying a house at a low price, investing money to make repairs and fix it up, and then reselling the house for a profit, all within a relatively short time frame – maybe 3 to 6 months. This is a best-case scenario. I can tell you from direct experience, however, that it doesn't always work out that neatly. If you're not careful and diligent, your rehab can take a lot longer than you planned, your rehab costs can far exceed your budget, and (trust me) there will always be unforeseen problems that come up (you've seen that happen on my TV show, *Flipping San Diego*).

If you think it's sexy to flip houses, let me clear one thing up. It's not. What's sexy is the big, fat paycheck that you get at the end of the flip, assuming that all went according to plan. In rehabbing, being a pessimistic optimist is a benefit (**Bedgoodism #11: Being a Pessimistic Optimist Can Be A Good Thing**). I am able to plan for the worst but hope for the best. This goes back to when I was a private mechanic, having to anticipate problems ahead of time so the plane wouldn't fall out of the sky. I've taken this into my rehabbing business and have learned to anticipate problems with flipping houses.

My definition of rehabbing: Taking a rough diamond and polishing it up, or taking a piece of coal and turning it into a diamond. Both require work and vision. There are different levels of rehabbing. There are the "carpet and paint" houses that mainly need some cosmetic work and clean up to get them back on the market. Everyone wants those houses because there is generally less risk, the rehab cost is relatively low, and the turnaround can be fast. There's also not as much profit in those houses, but the short turnaround time could be a better R.O.T. Then there are the houses that need significant work, and these are my favorite! They've generally been neglected for a time and have bigger problems: foundational, structural, code violations, pest infestations, roof, septic, and on and on. Again, watch an episode of *Flipping San Diego*, and you will get the idea. In order to make the repairs and then bring these types of houses up to neighborhood standards it will involve more time, money, and energy. However, the profits can be significantly larger because you can usually get these houses for a low price and sell high.

As an experienced rehabber, I don't shy away from anything. If you've seen *Flipping San Diego* or followed me on Facebook, you know I welcome a challenge. If the deal is right in the beginning and I can work the numbers, I'll take it on. I have the experience to know when I can add value and make the numbers work in my favor. If you're just getting into rehabbing, turn to your mentor and those trusted resources in your network to make sure your risk will reap a reward. (By now you've been building your network to include people on whom you can rely for advice and guidance.) When you're flipping a house, it's all about the numbers, so don't be afraid to say no and walk away if the deal is not right (**Bedgoodism #13: Learn To Say No**). At first it may hurt to walk away from potential money, but when you understand all the factors and realize the risk outweighs the payoff, then you're making the smart, best decision for your business.

At this stage in your investment business you're starting to realize more options when you come across a potential deal. Now you can determine whether you want to try and wholesale the house or keep it for a rehab. It might be a discussion of whether you want to make $10,000 or so in a week or make $40-50,000 in six months if you decide to take on the risk and flip it. But believe me, as an investor, that's a great predicament to be in! Those numbers work in any business trying to go from rags to riches.

If you're ready to learn more details about rehabbing, go to www.VeteranFlipper.com or follow me on Facebook at www. facebook.com/ChrisBedgoodFlippingSanDiego.

What Type of Investor Will You Be?

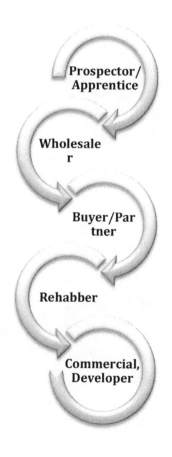

- Prospector/ Apprentice
- Wholesaler
- Buyer/Partner
- Rehabber
- Commercial, Developer

For the new investors reading this, I'll share one of my southern analogies with you (let me warn you, I'm going back to my Georgia roots for this one!).

"Don't get distracted by the dangling carrot and forget to stir the pot roast you already have cooking. Pay attention and make sure it comes out right."

What do I mean by that? Once you get established and networked, there will always be a carrot dangled in front of you. When you start to flip your first house and you have other leads flying into your email inbox or voicemail to take advantage of with subject lines like "Hot Wholesale DEAL, Hurry!" or a real estate agent that calls and says, *"A new deal just came on the MLS, we've got to hurry,"* etc., be careful and don't get distracted because a rehab you already have is underway. It can quickly go to hell if you are looking at your next potential deal and not paying attention to the one you already have. Be on-site once a day on your first deal, and control your destiny on your own house. I recommend not getting caught up in volume until you're ready to handle more. In order to handle more, you need systems. You need the right people, products, and processes. Tend to your first deal as you would tend to your pot roast. Hover over it; stir the pot. Don't let people who have other agendas control the outcome of your project. It may be tempting when you find a great deal on a property to think, I'm going to do this rehab myself, in three months, and make a fortune doing it." To that I say, *"Cool. Your. Jets."* Don't get overly confident because you heard some late night infomercial tell you that real estate investing is easy, and you can make $50,000 in 30 days. Don't be swayed from your cautious nature by these popular house flipping shows on TV that spotlight huge profits. Before you say anything, let me agree that these things can definitely happen! But we are experts at what we do. This isn't our first rodeo. But if it is yours, whoa, cowboy.

It is possible to make $50,000 in 30 days, and it is possible to make huge profits on your first house flip. But those scenarios are not the norm. If you go into this business basing your success on those events happening, you'll end up with an empty bank account or no deals under your belt. You could suddenly be chasing a rainbow. Instead, go into this business with your eyes and your ears open. Learn from others. Listen to what others are doing. Ask questions. Meet people. Determine what type of investor you want to be and determine your level of risk tolerance. Working with mentors, investor partners, and educators can serve as your safety net when taking on additional risk. It's nice to know they've got their eye on the success of the deal and of you, and can step in when needed.

When you are just getting started, it's ok to think about making tens of thousands of dollars a month, but for a new birddog, think about what an impact an additional $2,000, $3,000, or $5,000 a year could have on your life. How could increasing your income from $40,000/year to $50,000/year change how you live and the decisions you make? What if you could make an additional $2,000 to $5000 per month as a birddog? It's possible. But it starts with YOU. What amount of time are you willing to put into your real estate investing business? If you're still working a full-time job, you may want to begin by meeting other investors in your area and birddogging for them, earning a birddog fee on any deals you bring. That's something you can do while driving to and from work, in the evenings, or on weekends. It would mean little disruption to your life while building additional income. Are you already a successful birddog and ready to move to the next level, wholesaling? Have you built your network, are you getting more accustomed to the lingo and the process, and are ready to increase your risk tolerance? Are you ready to go all in and become a full-time investor?

No matter what stage you're in, go into it with your eyes open. Don't be swayed by what others are doing and don't get wrapped up in the excitement of a seminar or boot camp. The stakes are high – it's your reputation and possibly your own money. Be sure you're weighing all factors before jumping in.

Building Your Network

———————◆———————

Networking is critical to having your own Flags to Riches journey. It's about meeting people and telling others exactly what you are doing. It's the reason I'm where I'm at right now and continue to realize success in my business and my life.

Note: This whole section is about **Bedgoodism #5: Networking & Face Time**!

Networking is about letting other people know you exist. Do the things that other people may not consider to be networking. It's that extra thing that sets you apart from others. I call it "face time." If you're just getting started in real estate investing, you'll most likely start building your network from the ground up.

Where are the best places to network?

⇒ **REIA Meetings** – Check out a local Real Estate Investors Association meeting. Google it, or search on MeetUp to find one in your area. If there is more than one, check each of them out. The small amount of money you may need to pay to attend will be worth it in terms of the contacts you'll establish. Be sure to bring business cards and introduce yourself to the other attendees. Gather contact information and begin to build your list. Ask questions and keep your ears open to begin learning as much as you can. Check out my REIA at https://www.facebook.com/groups/SanDiegoREIA/ and at www.SanDiegoREIA.com.

⇒ **MeetUp Groups** – Go to www.meetup.com. Also check out my group at http://www.meetup.com/San-Diego-REIA-Real-Estate-Investors-Association/.

⇒ **Real Estate Investing Seminars or Boot Camps** – When I changed my mindset and was ready to boost my income, I started attending every investing seminar or boot camp that I could. I would travel to find them and do whatever I had to no matter what the admission fee. To me it was worth it to be in a room surrounded by like-minded people. These events are a great place to meet other investors.

⇒ **Mastermind Groups** – I've created and joined my share of mastermind groups, and I am a member of several. Mastermind groups bring together people who share the same focus, drive, and vision. They meet to motivate each other, solve problems, share information, and build their network. You may have to pay to join a mastermind group, but the investment you make will come back many times over.

⇒ **Facebook: Putting the Social in Social Media** – Facebook is a great tool for investors to use, both when you're just starting out and when you're an experienced investor. I've been using Facebook as a networking and marketing tool for years. I use it to not only share what's happening with my projects, but also to help sell properties or to find deals. It's an instant credibility builder, and credibility is KEY! *If you're not on Facebook talking about what's happening in your business, stop right now and set up your account. (But mark your place so you can come right back here!)* Even before I got the show *Flipping San Diego*, I would go to REIA meetings and people would know who I was when I walked into a room because I was very active on social media, specifically Facebook. How can you use Facebook, you ask? Use it to announce possible deals you have, to find other investors to wholesale to, to share photos of rehab projects – the before and (dramatic) afters, to post a house that you just put on the market, to announce a lead you came across. You're only limited by your imagination. You can link to videos on YouTube, even.

⇒ **Instagram** – If a picture is worth a thousand words, then before and after pictures are priceless. Take and post pictures of every house, even houses you've found that are just in the lead stage. Posting multiple properties creates credibility through volume. Everyone likes a good before and after story, and the uglier the start, the better the story. Don't be afraid to get creative with your hashtags, using things like #critterhousecrazyness or #crackhousemadness.

⇒ **YouTube** – Be your own mini-reality TV star or guru. Take people on the journey with you. Show them the ups and downs, create DRAMA, and use the footage for VALUE. Give educational moments. Post the 1 to 3 minute video clips on YouTube with catchy phrases, and people will not be able to resist but click on your video, "You won't believe what I found inside?" or "Accidental Indoor Pool."

There are tons of networking groups you can join beyond your local (and surrounding) REIA meetings. Get outside the norm and look at other types of networking where you can meet people. Groups like BNI or your Chamber of Commerce can be great places to meet people. Find out where the local real estate broker meetings are going on. Attend them, and always introduce yourself as a real estate investor. It only takes meeting one person to make attending worthwhile. But you have to get out there and let people know what you do. You have to *project* to the world what you do.

Networking is not instant. You have to build trust and one way is through face time (**Bedgoodism #5: Networking & Face Time**). It's not enough to just show up somewhere. You have to show up, shake people's hands, look them in the eye, and say, *"I'm Chris Bedgood. It's nice to meet you. I'm a real estate investor. What do you do?"* Except you will use your name instead of telling them you're Chris Bedgood! Soon, they will begin to know you, and they don't even know why! Before you know it, they're saying *"Hi, Chris. Nice to see you again."* If you get invited to something – some event – and those people are experienced or important or can provide value to you, you need to attend, even if it's only for a few minutes. Trust me, it's an awesome feeling when someone who can add value to your business calls you by your first name. It's this type of thing that will set you apart and put you in the 20% of successful business people rather than languishing in the other 80% trying to find their way.

Make sure you use the face time method at every seminar you attend. Always introduce yourself to the speakers and/or to the "important" people in the room. I would guess less than 20% of the attendees introduce themselves to the speaker or important people in the room! The other 80% lost a huge opportunity to create some face time. But don't just use it as a chance to talk about your latest deal. Just make it short and sweet. *"Hi Mr. Speaker. I'm Chris Bedgood. Great talk you just gave. Very informative and inspirational. I'm happy to be here and look forward to the rest of the event."* Wait for their courteous response, try to shake their hand, look them in the eye to show your confidence, and then move away. Short and sweet, but powerful if done correctly.

In networking, especially with speakers or mentors, a little goes a long way. Then make it a point to face time with them several more times during the event, especially at the end. Thank them for a great event with great content. Maybe bring up a particular comment they made and get a dialogue going, something that keeps them interested. Don't bring up your cracked foundation on your latest rehab. BORRRRIN-NNG!

*"Give positive energy to the person you're having face time with…
don't suck the life out of them!"*

Get them engaged so that they are staring at your face, getting that face time. Then if you see them again in two weeks or two months or if you see them on Facebook, they are much more likely to remember you and begin to bond with you, which could put you in their 20% of interesting people to talk to rather than the other 80% that they DON'T want to talk to. The key to this strategy is to think of it this way: if you didn't create face time with this mentor at this time or this event but other people did, you could be months behind those people. Get to know who the big players are. I always find out who the big players are in the room because I want them to respect me and bring me into their world. That's how I know my business will grow.

Networking still intimidates me; I have to make myself do it. It actually gives me anxiety. I'm not good at small talk. I HATE IT. But I force myself because I remind myself of the 80/20 rule. So do your face time and make it brief. It's like the 7-Touch Rule in sales; the theory is a prospective buyer needs to hear your message seven times before they will buy from you. The same principle can apply to networking. A prospective member of your network needs to meet you seven times before they consider you part of their network.

Use the seven touches to create and nurture the bond. We were all single at one time in our lives. My theory is, it's kind of like using the take away on a potential date you meet at a party, being elusive and enticing to others. A little mystery is enticing and interesting. Telling them everything about you at your first encounter or telling a guru your first wholesale or rehab during your first meeting is not fun or intriguing. It may be memorable, but not necessarily in a good way. This is **Bedgoodism #15: Learn The "Take Away,"** a little mystery goes a long way. It has served me well over the years and continues to even to this day. Just remember to ask about the other person, ask how they're doing. Create a dialog that makes that person remember you. You have to be different and stand out. You'll do that by being yourself, being genuine, and showing interest in them.

Connecting with Real Estate Brokers and Agents on Market Deals/MLS

Every successful real estate investor needs to build a network, a team of people who can make deals happen, a team of people you know will get the job done. Real estate agents or Realtors are essential members of your team. When you're building your network, you're definitely going to want to find a real estate agent who is investor-friendly and one whom you trust. Agents spend every day working with homebuyers and sellers. They are out in the neighborhoods talking with people, and they have their fingers on the pulse of what is happening in a given area.

That being said, I'm going to throw this out there, and it may not sound very positive on the surface, but here it is… real estate brokers do not have your best interest in mind. Before all the agents reading this get upset, please remember that I am a licensed agent myself so let me explain. I promise it will make you think. There is a fundamental difference in the thought process of real estate agents vs. real estate investors. Real estate brokers are salespeople. Financially speaking, they are focused on sales. And their income is based on commissions and R.O.T. (Return On Time). How much commission will I get in return for my time? Whereas financially speaking, real estate investors are focused on profits and R.O.I. How much return will I get on my money invested?

I remember a conversation I had with a broker about a flip house I was selling. The broker wanted me to drop my price.

"It's only a price reduction of $10,000." To me, that's $10,000 out of my pocket. To the broker, it's a fraction of that since a real estate agent gets a commission on the *total* sale. Let's do the math. If I'm selling a house for $300,000 that I spent $30,000 remodeling and $200,000 on the purchase, I want as much money back as possible. The agent's commission on a $300,000 home at 2.5% is $7,500. If I reduce my sales price by $10,000 to $290,000, then their commission goes down to $7,250. Only $250 difference! Whereas I have given up a whopping $10,000 in R.O.I. See the difference in mindset? This is important to understand because it shows the significance of you staying in control of your deals. Don't let the broker dictate the numbers or control your deal.

If you've done your due diligence and your own homework, you're not relying solely on what someone else is telling you that may impact your business – and your bank account – by thousands and thousands of dollars. Now don't get me wrong. I have worked hard as a licensed agent. Agents are a necessary and valuable part of your team. The good ones work very, very hard for you and deserve every penny that they receive. Treat them well and you will be rewarded many times over. Treat them bad and you can lose lots of opportunity in the future. In my network, I have a real estate agent angel whom I will call Alicia. She works for an REO broker, and she is my "in." When I first met her, I called her office off of a sign. I portrayed myself as a cash investor and said I needed to buy five houses a month and I still needed three more, and I didn't have a broker to write my offer. After keeping in contact with her and learning more about her business while sharing what I needed from her, we were able to embark on a long-term, lucrative (for both of us) relationship.

When you connect with real estate agents, keep in contact with them. When you call an agent, you may not make an offer, but try to get in some face time and meet and begin to bond with them, show you can perform, speak the language. You'll help them with their business while they help with yours. When I was a real estate agent, if I got a call on a house, I would go and meet the buyer. Once the buyer has met you, if you've done your job right, there is a bond. When I put on my investor hat, I thought, "How do I get brokers to believe in me?" It's not by door knocking or by sending out mailers; brokers have done that already. It's by meeting the brokers, either to make an offer or to ask them to send me properties. I will find where the broker is having an open house and meet them there to get some very valuable face time.

These are some simple things that you can start doing right now to build your network, and just maybe find your own real estate agent angel!

Connecting with Sellers

———•◆•———

The Hidden Market

I want to take a minute to talk about "the hidden market," or deals that do not come from real estate brokers, meaning they are not listed. I do most of my deals through real estate brokers and agents because that's the way I built my business. I created relationships and the deals now flow to me. I have the deal types and volumes I want. I know the type of investor I am, and if a deal comes to me that I don't want, I know how to lock it up and assign it to someone who does. You may not have the pipeline yet, so you need to tap in to all the deal resources around you. In addition to connecting with brokers, you will want to connect directly with sellers. One giant deal source is properties that are not listed. We call that the *hidden market*.

There are people all across America in situations where their properties need to be sold but they can't even afford to have a broker. Or they don't have the money necessary to fix the property enough for it to move on the retail market, the MLS. Or they don't have the time to wait for it to be marketed and sold and wait for closing on a conventional loan. That's where you come in. Remember how I told you my agents bring me deals before they market them because they know I close quickly? How would you like to market for people in the situations I listed above and have them call you direct because you advertise that you can close quickly (with the added bonus of no broker commissions)? Well, marketing to motivated homeowners is the key. Motivated homeowners are people who are short on time, short on money, no longer want the property, are in probate, became accidental landlords when they weren't able to sell their homes in the crash, are in transition, are going through a divorce, relocation, or even have expanding families. I could go on and on, but you get the idea.

By putting up signs like the one in the back of my car that said "CASH 4 Houses," letting people know simply, "I BUY HOUSES CASH" or "QUICK CASH FOR YOUR HOME," motivated sellers will call you. You can also send letters, postcards, put up door hangers, and much more. Once the calls come in, you can evaluate the deal, prospect it, assign it, or buy it yourself, depending on where you are at in your investor lifecycle and who is calling. These are the best homes to market and prospect or assign since there are fewer people involved in the deal and often there is more room for negotiation and opportunity for discounts due to the condition of the home and/or need for speed.

I want to be clear that we never take advantage of anyone. Everyone gets a fair offer for their property; we are here to help, never to hurt. It's happened many times that people I know in this business have helped by purchasing someone's problem property quickly and then been referred to the seller's friends and family. Word of mouth is the best form of marketing.

Understanding Deal Criteria

———•◆•———

When you're looking for properties to buy, whether as a birddog, wholesaler, investor partner, or rehabber, you will want to look for certain criteria – signs that will indicate whether a property has the potential to be a good "deal" or not. Let me preface this section by saying one thing. What works for me in San Diego may not be exactly what works for you in your area. The things I look for aren't necessarily what others look for in their state or city or even in another country. That's why it's important to listen, learn, and do your homework. Talk to brokers and other investors *in your area*. Find out what's selling, what people are looking for, and what other investors are looking for (especially when you're a birddog or wholesaler).

Pay attention to things like:

⇒ Zip codes.

⇒ Number of beds/baths.

⇒ When the houses were built.

⇒ Types of homes.

⇒ Neighborhood surroundings.

⇒ Accessibility.

⇒ Whether the house is on city utilities.

There is one over-arching piece of advice I will give: **Don't choose the neighborhood. Choose the deal.** In San Diego County, the neighborhoods are diverse. There can be a house with a beautiful ocean view located right in the heart of a gang territory. I have purchased houses in not-so-great neighborhoods in the past, but I don't automatically jump on those deals; the numbers really have to be right. It's a risk tolerance thing (**Bedgoodism #9: Know Your Risk Tolerance**).

I work with houses in the $100,000 to $1 million range. This wide span is possible because I have built my business to be able to handle many different price ranges. As a new rehabber or flipper, you may want to have your criteria lower, maybe $25,000 to $400,000, so you aren't getting bogged down running numbers on property you can't even handle. A cluttered email inbox with leads you can't flip and don't have time to analyze can kill your R.O.T. Remember, your market will dictate the price point, *and* your experience as a birddog, your risk tolerance, and your network of buyers will also help you determine the price point you start with. As you and your systems grow, so can your reach. As I mentioned earlier, as a birddog, don't shy away from anything. When you come across a lead, turn it over to someone in your network. As a wholesaler, if you have a diverse list of investors in the network you've built, as long as the numbers work, don't shy away from any potential deals.

For a rehabber, the numbers really do have to work. I generally will focus on a 3 bed, 2 bath house because my buyer pool is larger. More importantly, I look for houses that I can add value to such as a 2 bed, 1 bath that I can turn into a 3/2 without adding square footage. I also look for indicators that might exclude a large percentage of potential buyers. For example:

⇒ Houses without a garage.

⇒ Houses on a busy street or without a yard will eliminate families with small children.

⇒ Houses with a second story will eliminate elderly buyers or those with a handicap.

⇒ Houses with obsolete floor plans that don't allow good 'flow' or Feng Shui.

When you're looking for properties, it will be important, really important, to know the "comps" of your house. "Comps" are the comparables in the neighborhood and will tell you what similar houses in the area have sold for in the past. To find out this information, you will need to somehow have access to the MLS (Multiple Listing Service) – either yourself or through a trusted real estate broker. Don't rely on popular home listing websites like Zillow. While those sites are great for finding out some basic information, they are not as detailed and comprehensive as the MLS. When you run comps, make sure you are comparing apples to apples. Find similar houses in terms of number of beds/baths, square footage, and any special amenities (like a pool) to the property you're comparing. If you need to extend the radius of your search, then do so in order to get the most accurate comparison. Knowing the comps in the area will give you an idea of the resale value of your target property; it will give you a ballpark figure that you can expect. This will help provide a basis for your offer or a starting point for your negotiation.

One word of caution: avoid falling in love with a house. Having that strong connection can cloud your judgment and the decisions you'll make on the deal. If the numbers don't work or if the property is just too big of a headache, wholesale it or say no and walk away. I HATE walking away from potential deals, but I love keeping my bank account full rather than writing checks to get out of bad deals that I never should have bought in the first place. Remember, what works for me may not necessarily work in your area, so make sure you're networking, asking questions, and learning. Talk to other investors who are having success in your area. Wholesale THEM your difficult, potentially migraine-causing deals. Work with your trusted mentor to find out the best formula for your area.

Finding Deals and Sellers: Marketing Strategies

---◆---

As a real estate investor, your business will revolve around finding deals and beating others to the punch. When I first started getting serious about becoming a full-time investor, I tried many different forms of marketing to find deals and people who were interested in selling or who "needed" to sell their house. Some marketing strategies were more successful than others, and over time, I was able to focus my time and energy on the ones that paid off the most (**Bedgoodism #6: Measure Your Return On Time**), the low hanging fruit, as I like to say. Below are just some of the strategies I used to find deals and sellers:

1. **Mailers** – I got title reps to help me locate people who lived in other states that might want to sell their property, and I sent mailers to them trying to get my phone to ring.

2. **60 to 90 Day Lates** – I searched for people who were 60 to 90-days late on their payments through tax records and door knocking. This meant researching the tax records and then physically driving to their house, knocking on

their door, and asking them if I could talk with them about buying their house before it went to foreclosure.

3. **Bandit Signs** – I hung bandit signs all over San Diego. I bought a staple gun and hung signs that said "We Buy Houses" with my phone number on it and posted them around town.

4. **Hand Written Letters** – I also wrote letters that said, "I am looking to buy a house in your neighborhood, and I love your house. Please call if you are interested in selling."

5. **Driving for Dollars** – I *drove for dollars*, meaning I drove around town looking for houses that were dilapidated and tried to track down the owner by talking to neighbors or mailing a letter to them, or even leaving a note on their door.

6. *Cash 4 Houses* **Signs** – I put a cardboard sign in the back window of my car that said *"Cash 4 Houses"* in big blue letters with my phone number on it. People would stop me at gas stations and wherever they might see me. I then would give them my card or get their information and call or follow up later.

7. **Realtor Signs** – I started calling FOR SALE signs when I would be driving around neighborhoods. Of course I wanted to try to make an offer on the house, but mainly I was trying to connect with the agent (remember the 7-Touches Rule?). I would explain that I was an investor, get myself on their buyer's list, and try to find out about their properties *before* they hit the market. I would then follow up and hope to get a deal down the road.

8. **Fellow Investors** – Always let other investors know what you're doing. They can be a great resource. Not all investors are looking for the same types of properties, so if you let other investors know what you're doing, you're increasing the odds that they will call you when they have a property they are not interested in.

No matter what, make sure you have plenty of business cards to hand out. Nothing elaborate – just something with your name, phone number, and email address and something like, *"Cash 4 Houses."* Give them to everyone you meet, along with some extras for them to share. I've had success with getting leads from all of these techniques and more. Plus there are many other strategies that I don't have time to cover here. These are working (or have worked) for me. Find *your* best way to market. Find the method that keeps you interested and gives you the strongest R.O.I. and R.O.T.

All of these marketing techniques can and do work. It is up to you to get out of bed every day and implement the methods you choose. It is up to you to decide how bad you want it.

Understanding Why Seasons Are Important in Real Estate

I want to take a quick minute to talk about seasons in real estate investing and why seasons can play a big role in your investing outcome. Depending on the time of year, you may find more properties coming on to the market, more homes selling, more buyer traffic, more seller traffic, or fewer homes selling and less traffic. The time of year can play a huge role in what's happening in the housing market and by default, what you may be able to expect in your own business and the profits on your deals. Think about it. Cold, snowy winter months bring renewed energy in spring. Summer vacations. What's going on with buyers and sellers will reflect in what's happening in life.

If you're going to undertake a rehab project, it can be ideal to buy at the end of the year, work on your rehab during the winter months and have the property ready to put on the market for the spring buyers. Birddogs can bring leads to other investors at any time of the year. The same is true for wholesalers. You will be able to sell a house any time if your buyer's list is deep enough and varied enough. You'll have investors who will want vacant lots, those who buy and hold, flip, buy and hold and flip later, and so on. But if you're flipping houses, you need to be very aware of seasons. I love to buy houses in November or December. Asset managers are eager to get the properties off their books, people aren't looking at houses, and many investors go dormant during that time of year.

If you're buying and are looking at a basic "carpet and paint" rehab, where the work will mainly be cosmetic, then you can buy in May and get it on the market in June, during prime selling season. But if you buy a house in May that has a cracked slab or other major problems and may need two to three months, plus permits, to complete the work, your house will not be ready to go on the market until August or September, which is traditionally a time for vacations and back-to-school. If you buy in November or December and list in February or March, you have the potential to get a great deal on the house and get it on the market in time for the spring selling season.

You will want to adjust your purchase price according to the seasons. If you're buying at the end of the year, you will be able to make a more aggressive offer. October and November are riskier times to sell, and you'll need to account for that in the budget or wholesale it or walk away. If you wait it out, you may need to factor in additional holding costs. In addition to the weather and months on the calendar, take into account what's happening in society (like a presidential election, the last one killed the market because everyone was in wait-and-see mode).

If you have a good product, you will be able to sell your house during any season. But be sure to factor all these things into your overall budget, plan for it, and then roll the dice. Again, while each house you buy or sell will be different, understanding how seasons impact the buying and selling patterns will give you an extra edge.

Making the Offer

---◆---

By the time you're ready to make an offer on a property, you've done your due diligence. You've looked at the property, you've run your comps, asked questions, and you've determined approximately what the rehab costs will be (this is important whether you're wholesaling or planning on rehabbing the house yourself).

Now you're ready to make an offer. Let's look at some tips to successful offer making.

⇒ Make offers quickly. Good deals won't wait two weeks for you to do your due diligence.

⇒ Know your highest offer, but don't start it with it and NEVER go above it.

⇒ Use a solid contract. Protect yourself with an exit clause that covers clear title, a right to inspect, the ability to assign, and partner approval.

⇒ If an offer does not get accepted, schedule it for follow up. Check again in two weeks, 30-days, etc. until the property sells. Time creates motivation in real estate.

⇒ *Always* thank everyone for their time.

⇒ Work with your attorney, mentor, real estate brokers, and other trusted team members.

⇒ As you grow and take deals on yourself, close deals at your title company whenever possible to enjoy the benefits you've secured by being a good repeat client.

Funding Your Deals Using Other People's Money (O.P.M.)

---◆---

One of the most important things you'll need for a successful deal is access to funds. You will have to show proof of funds, meaning you have the money to back up your offer. When you're just starting out this may seem like the hardest part, but in reality, it's not. Don't let the fear of finding funds hold you back from doing a deal.

There are many ways to fund your real estate deals, but my favorite is using O.P.M. (Other People's Money). The two most common ways to use O.P.M. are through hard money lenders or private money lenders. Of course you can use your own money or go to a bank and get a conventional loan, but both of those methods come with drawbacks and limitations. Even in these cases, you'll need to show proof of funds to show you have money in the bank. Here, I'm going to focus on using O.P.M. through private lenders because they are my favorite.

When you're making offers on the MLS, know that nine times out of ten you'll have to provide a proof of funds before your offer will get accepted. But how do you get proof of funds?

When you use O.P.M., one way is to use your lender's proof of funds. Finding private money lenders goes back to your networking and making connections with money people. You'll meet potential lenders at REIA meetings, seminars, masterminds, or in other networking organizations. Your potential lender may be another investor. It may be someone who is not an active investor but has money they want to invest in real estate such as a doctor, attorney, or a business owner who wants a better R.O.I. than his or her bank or stocks.

When you approach an investor for their money or their proof of funds, you're entering into a negotiation. You might offer to pay or compensate them to use their proof of funds, and this fee can be negotiable. Don't be afraid to ask or to get creative. For example, when I was getting started, I worked a deal with another investor where I used his proof of funds, and we agreed upon an 80/20 split on the profits (80% to him and 20% to me), but I also served as project manager on the rehab and would also receive the commission on the resale of the property as the listing agent. Everything can be overcome; you just need to think creatively. A troubleshooter sees a problem and figures out a way to solve it.

The easiest access to funding deals is by going to REIA club meetings. It's a great place to problem solve, put your heads together, and find funding to buy, sell, or rehab. One of my favorite REIAs is the San Diego Creative Investors Association or SDCIA (www.SDCIA.com). It has "creative" right in the name because real estate investing is all about getting creative to get deals done. Henry Ford was a visionary when it came to cars, but what he was even better at was surrounding himself with people who were smarter than him who could turn his vision into reality. To be successful at real estate investing, you have to realize that you don't have to do everything on your own. You just need to surround yourself with people who can help get you to the next level. If you can adopt that mindset, it will take a lot of the pressure off of you. You need to think like Henry Ford so you can grow rich!

If you're using other people's money for your investment deals, chances are they will tell you if a deal is a good one or if it's not. Most lenders, especially hard money lenders, have "red flags" or criteria that they use because they know where the risk lies. It's good to have your lender look at a deal because they can tell you what they think and where to be careful. Remember, when you have a mentor and/or are part of a network, they can play different roles in the deal. As a birddog you may have brought in leads, as a wholesaler sold the leads; now as a rehabber you may find yourself going back to the same people and partnering on deals or even using them as private lenders. They have watched you grow, so if the asset looks good and the trust and credibility is there, the money will chase good people with good deals, naturally.

Leads vs. Deals (You Can't Spell DEALS without LEADS)

I touched on this earlier but want to focus on it again so you really understand the difference of these two very important terms. For birddogs just starting out, it is important to know and understand the difference between leads and deals. Birddogs will spend time chasing leads and handing them off to investors who might be able to turn them into deals. Wholesalers take leads and turn them into deals. Investors take deals and turn them into profit.

A lead is a "maybe." It's not that scary. It has no merit or numbers to it yet. It's just something that might be able to be turned into a deal. It might be a phone number to a seller, but nothing concrete. A deal is something more solid. It has merit. That phone number has a seller at the end of it who wants to sell the house and is motivated, and the numbers look decent. That is a potential deal that an experienced investor can work with. Leads are important, but they need to be filtered through quickly to determine if they can be turned into a deal or tossed in the trash.

A lead may not go anywhere, but when you get a deal accepted and it starts to actually happen, that's exciting and scary because now you have something tangible to work with that requires you to get creative and perform. I remember the first time I turned a lead into a deal. I was excited and scared out of my pants because I knew I had found my first potential real estate payday, but now how was I going to turn it into money? My fear was losing the deal I just found. What do I do now? But in this business, fear is a good thing. Even now, every time I get an offer accepted, I experience a bit of fear. That's healthy. It means you're doing what other people are not, and you're living outside of your box, outside of your comfort zone. And that's why I turn to my mentors when I find a deal that scares me. To this day I have mentors that I will ask questions to get their feedback before I roll the dice or make a big decision.

Here's a bit of extra Bedgood wisdom: *Be careful about borrowing money from family and close friends on your very first deal.* Honestly, I don't recommend it (in the beginning). Learn how to cook that pot roast and make it nice before bringing your friends and family to sit at the table with you. Get the kinks out on your first rehab before you invest your friends or family's money. The stress from worrying about a family member's money or having a friend hovering over your every move will kill your relationship. I've seen it happen. Be cautious and cool. If a family or friend is the *only* person who will do the deal with you after you've approached investors with it, then maybe you should walk away from the deal or wholesale it to a volume-based investor or a landlord portfolio buyer.

IMPORTANT: Be careful about long-term permanent or implied partnerships. Be wary of attaching yourself or "marrying" someone when it comes to investing, especially rehabbing. In my experience, partners may not always put in equal amounts to a project, and you can very easily have a falling out. Remember, real estate investing can change your life quickly, so there is a lot at stake. If you're a go-getter or type-A personality, it can be hard to hold other people accountable to your goals and standards.

If you *do* choose to enter into a partnership, make sure to write down exactly what each party will be expected to do, outline who does what and when, and draft a buy-out agreement if the relationship goes in a different direction. Remember, a contract is used when buying and selling real estate, so why wouldn't you have these same types of things in place when partnering. **Bedgoodism #7: Treat Your Daily Life Like A Business**, and you can't help but succeed.

I say this because it can be easy to get caught up in the excitement of a seminar or boot camp and want to partner with the person you've been sitting next to and have formed a friendship with. Or maybe with a contractor you have met who also wants to be an investor. Just use caution and go into the situation with your eyes open. You don't "need" *anyone.* Use that excitement to build your energy and drive you towards your goals, but don't let it blind you into making decisions you may regret later. My advice is to partner on one deal first or maybe have a 6 to 12-month agreement. If things go well after the first deal or trial period, the partners then revisit their partnership. Lives change. Mindsets change. Partnerships change. I recommend you NEVER partner long term. I recommend you partner PER DEAL, EVERY DEAL. Don't form corporations together. They are hard to dissolve. And if you do choose to partner, always have escrow do your vesting as *Tenants In Common.* Ask your escrow officer or real estate broker for more information on vesting; it is one of the most important details that you don't want to skip. I have plenty of strategies that I can share about how to successfully navigate an investing partnership, but I'll save those for another time. For now, just heed my advice for caution.

Deals Move Quickly!

In real estate investing, deals need to be made quickly. If you have everything lined up and in place, you'll be able to react and jump on a good opportunity when it arises. You're constantly moving money as an investor. Becoming an expert in funding deals comes with experience; I'm still learning. If you can't come up with the money, you will not only lose the deal, but you'll lose the trust from the real estate agent because they won't see you as an investor who can perform. Here's a scenario from when I was starting as an investor.

I got a call from a real estate agent with whom I had already bonded and formed a connection. She had a problem property that kept falling out of escrow and asked if I would be interested. I went to see the property. The house wasn't in bad shape so I was interested but I didn't have any money. What I did have was a cell phone, and I knew I wanted to make this deal happen. I knew I could use the tools I had at my disposal, so I started calling people I got to know through my networking. I thought the numbers on the house were good, so there was potential. I was scared to death! I could have just let it go and gone to the beach and forgotten about it, but I changed my mindset and was determined to find someone who would be able to help me. I had goals. I had a house right in front of me. I was going to make it happen.

I made an offer to the real estate agent and told her I was a cash buyer, but she needed to see proof of funds. While inside I was saying, *"Oh crap!"* outside I said, *"Sure, I'll get that for you."* So I called an investor I knew. I told him I had this house, told him the numbers, what I thought I could sell it for, and asked whether he wanted in on the deal. I said I would run the rehab project; he would approve everything, and be the final decision maker. I asked for a split on the net profit (20%) and a real estate broker commission for the resale. I explained that if he didn't get at least x amount back on this deal, I would forego my profit and just take the resale commission. He accepted the deal. Right then, I turned another page in my investing career. I asked for something more.

Don't scare away your investors – let them know their money is safe. I did this by explaining I would personally run the rehab, but he would have the final say in any decisions. By offering to forego my share of the profits if I didn't get a certain amount for the house, I was showing him that I was completely invested in making the deal a profitable one. Even though I wasn't investing my money directly, I was committed to making the deal a success. After this deal, the investor was more than willing to work with me again because he knew I would get him more deals, and he knew that I would do whatever I could to increase his R.O.I. He saw me as a new source of profit for him.

You have to go out and find private investors for your deals, and they're out there. It's your job to network, spread the word about what you're doing – tell everyone! Learn to ask questions and build a list of people you can talk to. When you bring a deal to a private money lender, make sure you've done your due diligence. Make sure you can show them their expected return on investment. That means running the comps, understanding what needs to be done on the house (repairs), understanding potential resale value. Don't just trust what a real estate broker might tell you; find out for yourself. Understand all this before you can expect someone to write you a check. Don't be afraid to negotiate your split with the investor. Once you find someone who is willing to give you their money (because you have proven yourself), you may stay with the same arrangement for a while. But as you progress, you may find the opportunity to renegotiate a different split. The investor I worked with whom I told you about earlier? After working with him on several deals, I renegotiated a 50/50 split on the net profit.

Make sure you have several private money lenders to work with. After a while, their lives may change, and their investing needs may change with it. There's no cookie-cutter method to follow. Each deal will be different so it's up to you to learn and listen, ask questions, and most importantly, build your network.

Case Study #3: Wholesaling with Other People's Money (63rd Street)

"I like to cultivate relationships with listing agents; not just agents who work mostly with buyers. Agents who get listings are in control of the listing and have direct access to the seller. This gives me an advantage over other investors because I am one step ahead of the information they have."

This is a property that was brought to me by a Realtor that I wholesaled to another investor. I had been working with this Realtor for a while and we developed a good rapport, so when she called, I always answered the phone (and still do!). She was my best birddog because I trained her to look for houses that I could flip. I taught her what I was and was not looking for. This agent called and said she had a good house, but it had weird add-ons and structures in the back. It was a solid, 3 bed, 2 bath and had a 1 bed, 1 bath detached house (a "granny flat") in the back that was not on tax records. She suggested I go look at the house. She could submit my offer before anyone else's, and maybe the bank would accept. Knowing I have to do what others won't do, which means get off my butt and get in my car and look at houses, I did just that, and I'm glad I did.

This house is located in a not-so-good part of San Diego, but in an area where houses are affordable and people would pay good money for a nice house. Plus it is a great rental area so there is always a chance for cash flow. This particular property had a chance for both, which can be rare. An unpermitted, one bedroom house (or apartment, for that matter) can be a good thing even if it is unpermitted or not in the tax records because buy and hold investors love these. Why? Because they are only paying for the permitted house and the land. The extra one bedroom house is pretty much free square footage, which means they can have another tenant and create cash flow without having to build another structure (Remember to learn the rules and regulations in your local market).

At the time I was not looking to hold any property. I wanted to make quick cash and wholesale properties like this. So I made an offer to the bank, and they accepted it (and my offer was *low*). Because of my relationships and the bank needing to get this property off their books and because they knew I would perform, I got it!

If you aren't a little uncomfortable or embarrassed when you make an offer then you've probably offered too much.

Woo hoo! Or actually, OMG... now what do I do? I didn't have the money to close on this property. I took pictures of the property. I analyzed what it would take to get it rent-ready, as well as what it would take to flip the property. I inspected the house to see if there were any major defects and what the positives and negatives were so that I could properly present this house to potential investors who would pay me a finder's fee (wholesale assignment fee). (Be sure to know the rules and regulations in your market.)

This was a true wholesale because I actually had it under contract in my corporation's name. This can be risky if you are unable to come up with deposit money or unable to find an investor because if you have to cancel, then you've not only hurt your reputation, but you've hurt your real estate agent's reputation with her bank and the asset manager. If that happens, it's unlikely you will ever get first dibs at one of her listings again. You will go to the end of her top 10 list instead of the number one position. Don't let that happen. Provide as much information to your investors as you can so they can make a quick decision. Remember, every day you have this property tied up is another day that your contingency periods are getting eaten up, and there is the possibility of you losing your deposit. I was unable to get an investor to put up the deposit for me in the allotted 3-day period, so I had to put up the $3,000 deposit myself. Generally it is *not* difficult to borrow $3,000 to tie up a property. Make a deal with a family member or someone you know to pay them a little return on their money, usually 10%. You would then make your investor reimburse you the $3,000, *plus* the 10% to whomever you borrowed the money from. This is another way to use only O.P.M. If you were able to find a lender for the $3,000 but were unable to close and decided to cancel the escrow, then escrow would refund the $3,000 back to you, and then you would have to pay your lender back plus interest, if that is what you worked out.

Regardless, get creative. There are *tons* of ways to borrow money for short periods from people who believe in you. **(Bedgoodism #14: Find People Who Believe In You... And Leave The Others Behind)** Find those people. Always be projecting and letting people know what you do so that one day when you call someone to borrow money, they won't be surprised to hear that you are a real estate investor. Even if you've never done a deal or received a birddog fee or completed a wholesale, you should still tell everyone that you are a real estate investor. This will keep you accountable and keep you focused.

I ended up finding an investor for this property. He happened to be a pretty good friend of mine whom I had met a couple years earlier when I was a real estate agent. I helped him find properties until one day I took my agent hat off and put my investor hat on. He was now going to pay me a fee for finding him a deal; it was good for both of us. After all expenses, I made about $14,000 on that deal in 30 days with only two visits to the actual property and multiple emails and phone calls. I call that a pretty good R.O.T. (Return on Time)!

What I learned from that deal is I don't like putting up my own deposit money. I like to use the investor's money when I can. I learned to have smaller investors who could lend small amounts of money for short periods of time. I learned to have my investor pay back my deposit as soon as possible while still in escrow so that I could get that money back. I also wholesaled my first property that could be used as a rental, which allowed me to reach a new type of investor and have different types of properties on my radar.

Case Study #4: The House No One Wanted Made Me $38,000 (Van Dyke St.)

This property scared the heck out of me and gave me a few migraines, but that intrigues me and allows me to grow. This is a classic, do what others won't do situation. A get-outside-my-comfort-zone type of thing. A keep-you-up-at-night type of thing.

I got a call from a local wholesaler. He couldn't unload this property, which made me a little wary. It was a hot market for investors picking up property, so why wouldn't they buy it. My initial thought was it would be a waste of my time. I need to focus on properties that make sense. He told me he wanted $119,000 for the house. That is a great price point in any area of San Diego and deserved a second look. This wholesaler had wanted to do a deal with me for a while and we just couldn't seem to come together on our numbers. I asked if $119,000 was his final price. He said it was. He was dropping it for me because he knew if I said yes, I wouldn't back out like other investors had done. This was a chance to pick up a deal, create another relationship, prove that I can perform, and possibly get another lender under my belt. I wanted to move on from my other lender who was turning down deals. I needed to go to the next level. So I looked at the house, and it was a doozy, to say the least.

On tax records it was a 600-ish square foot, 2 bed, 1 bath. But in actuality it had several weird rooms and add-ons (extra, unpermitted square footage) that added up to another 400 square feet! And it had a garage, which was a huge bonus. The extra square footage looked like it had been well done and that it had been added many, many years ago, probably at least 50 years ago. My design mind was racing; maybe I could convince an FHA appraiser to give me a boost for the square footage. Two bed, 1 bath, 600-750 sq. ft. houses without garages (remodeled) were selling for $215,000 to $225,000.

As I inspected the exterior, I saw why everyone was walking away from this house. The exterior walls seemed as if they were folding like a house of cards. This told me the house had major structural issues. The house was on a raised foundation, but someone had poured a two-inch layer of leveling concrete on top of it and then laid ceramic tile on the entire floor throughout the house. So the walls were out of plumb, and the foundation couldn't support the weight of the floor. On top of that the roof was bad, the electrical was bad, the plumbing was shot, the landscaping was completely overgrown to where you couldn't see the house from the street, and the floor plan was awful. How could I make this work? I decided I would make it work, but the numbers worried me.

I called my new lender and got him to see the house. He saw it, and now he was worried, too. Instead of doing a 50/50 split, he wanted a guaranteed return, meaning no matter what happened with the sale, he would receive a guaranteed pay day, and I would receive whatever was left over, if any. If I were to royally mess up, he would take over the property, and I would owe him. But I now had a lender who was willing to give me money. The numbers were there. Even if I messed up, I could see that he would get his money back, and I might walk away with a great lesson. But that's not how I run my business. I don't run it on hope or maybe I can. I had more due diligence to figure out. I called out a contractor that I knew would understand this house. He was not cheap, but I knew his bid would be solid and that he wouldn't charge me for overages at every turn. He looked at the house and told me he could fix it, but recommended I walk away. I took his comments very seriously. I was sweating. Anxious. I had told my wholesaler friend that I was going to close on this house. He had reserved it for me at a great deal. But I couldn't buy a property that was too difficult, or could I?

I felt my, go over the wall, around the wall, under the wall, or through the wall mentality kicking in. But I also needed to be smart. I wanted to be a successful investor who receives checks. Not a guy who has to write a check at the end of a project because he didn't buy it right or give himself a cushion for changes and overages.

Out of curiosity, I called up my wholesaler buddy and asked him, "What if I cancel on you? What is that going to do to our relationship, and what will happen to the property?" He replied, "I won't send you any more properties, and I will lose my deposit on this one." (New investors should really be cautious. Don't let another investor's issues become yours even if someone says this to you. It's not your fault he has gotten a bad property under contract and doesn't want to close on it. It's better to walk away than fail miserably and go bankrupt on your first house, or your fiftieth, for that matter). This house was seemingly too risky for me, with too many problems and unknowns. But, I had a moment of inspiration, a moment of "think outside the box." Think, design, and make some money.

I went back to the property again and met my contractor. I asked him, can we turn this 2 bed, 1 bath into a 3 bed, 1 ¾bath *(3/4 means it is a shower bathroom with no tub, which is fine in master bedrooms. I recommend you always have one tub in the house, but that one tub should be a public or hall bathroom, not the master.)*? My contractor and I spent a couple of hours measuring the house, inspecting everywhere. We measured and laid out a completely new floor plan that would require removing every interior wall in the house. We scratched stuff out, remeasured over and over again, moving walls, adding baths, removing windows, adding windows, etc. It was almost there but we just couldn't quite fit it. But then my "Never Give Up" design mindset came in. That nagging, never fail, figure this out, no one cares about this but you mentality. And then I figured it out. I asked my contractor if we could make the kitchen a little smaller, which would make the master bedroom a little bigger. He said, "Hmmm… Well…Hmmm. Umm. Well, let's look at that." He measured some more. Went into the attic. Finally he said it will cost you a little more in some structural work, but yes, we can move that wall and I can re-support the roof, blah, blah, blah. All I heard was "YES." I can do that, and all it will cost me is a little MONEY. I had just figured it out! We would change the entire floor plan and create a master bedroom with its own ¾ shower bathroom with a tiny sink and toilet, all barely fitting to code and usable. *(When designing always think about local codes, but don't forget about flow and usability. Imagine yourself living there and design accordingly.)* He also had a plan to fix the house of cards by tearing out every piece of drywall in the house, including the ceilings, rebuilding the walls, fixing the cause of the swaying walls, breaking out all the concrete floor and tile, repairing the foundation, and moving all the walls around in the house.

Design, architectural drawings, engineering, and permitting took a while, but this house turned out to be a game changer for me. I created a great relationship with a new lender. I created a better relationship with a wholesaler whom I've purchased many more deals from since and will continue to. I learned a heck of a lot. I bought the property for $119,000 plus some closing costs. I spent $68,000 on the remodel and sold the property for $265,000. After paying off the lender and all the re-sale closing costs, I walked away with a $35,000 net profit *without using my own money* because the lender paid all the costs, including the remodel. I was able to get much more for the house because we changed it from a 2 bed, 1 bath, 600 square foot house into a 1,000 square foot, 3 bed, 2 bath house. I had vision, and vision is what will separate you from other investors.

In real estate flipping I'm always looking for the "pain." What is paining the seller or wholesaler? Why would they want to get away from this house, and how can I use that to my advantage in my negotiations? Pain can mean a paycheck, if I can get it for the right price. But a seller's pain can also mean a migraine for me. Every other investor was cancelling on this wholesaler because they couldn't figure this property out. It was too risky and priced too high. I needed to go to the next level. The point in this story is I had to get outside my comfort zone and force myself to go to the next level. I've found that the best deals are the ones that nobody else wants.

Negotiation

———————◆———————

Y ou can negotiate at virtually every stage of your investing journey and at almost every stage of the deal process,
even if you're just starting out. Everything can be overcome;
you need to think creatively.

As a birddog, you can begin to negotiate your fee. When you
approach an investor with a lead, he or she may offer to assign you a fee if the dry lead turns into a deal. If, over time,
you've brought multiple leads to that investor that turn into
deals, and you begin to emphasize the value you can bring to
that investor, you may feel comfortable negotiating a higher
fee. If the investor was paying you $500 per lead, you may
now ask for $1,000 (I'll say it one more time, it's important to
know rules and regulations in your own market.).

By practicing your negotiation skills, you will increase your
confidence. And in this business, you need to have a LOT
of confidence. Real estate investors want to work with other
confident people – and that might mean bringing a little bit
of attitude! I told you when I was getting started I negotiated
an 80/20 split with another investor and would manage the
rehab project and get the selling commission on the listing. I

not only negotiated that deal, but the more deals we did together and the more value he saw in what I could bring to his business, I was eventually able to negotiate a 50/50 split on profits (but no selling commission).

Negotiating with other investors is just the start of it. As I said, you can negotiate at virtually every step in the investing process:

⇒   Your birddog fee.

⇒   Your contract assignment fee.

⇒   Your profit split with another investor.

⇒   Fee for using another investor's proof of funds.

⇒   Commission structure with your real estate broker.

⇒   Negotiate with your contractors ("Let me think about it, I can do better.").

⇒   Perhaps most importantly, negotiating on the buy and sell price of a house.

Negotiating on the purchase or sale of a property can be a real art form. We don't have enough time or space to cover every detail or strategy here in this book. But what I will do is hit some of the highlights. When you're buying a property, it's essential that you do your due diligence and learn as much as you can about the property, the rehab needs (whether you're going to wholesale it or rehab it yourself), and the comps. With this knowledge, you'll be able to determine your overall investment, exit strategy, and potential net profit. After you've targeted a property as a potential investment deal, find out the asking price. That number will most likely not be the amount you will get it for. Go to the house and conduct your own inspection. Make note of the condition and ball-park possible repair costs. Run your comps and then determine your offer. There are some standard formulas that you can use. Check with your mentor to find out the best ones for your area and for your level of risk tolerance.

Follow Up

———————◆———————

Follow-up is going to be one of the most important things you can do to advance your investing business. It is the one thing that can separate you from the other investors. In fact, because of thorough follow-up alone, I am able to add another 10+ houses to my investment portfolio each year. Having a good follow-up system is one thing that can set you apart from other investors. When you're looking for properties, just because a house is listed on the MLS as "Pending" doesn't mean it's a done deal. Houses fall out of escrow all the time, and if you're watching and monitoring what is happening, you just may be the one to jump in and take over when it does happen. If you are able to connect with the listing agent and create a bond with him or her, you may be able to gain some insight into what's happening with the sale of a house. If a "Pending" house does go back on the market, that agent will be more likely to reach out and offer you the opportunity to make an offer. Why? Because you've been following up and keeping in touch with the agent. If you've successfully created a bond, the agent will know that you are a performer and will be able to close on the deal.

Successful networking involves diligent follow-up, too. When you meet other investors or potential private money lenders at REIA club meetings or seminars, make sure to follow up with them. Ask questions about their business and keep your ears open for potential opportunities. If you're positioning yourself as a birddog, follow through by bringing them leads. If you're a wholesaler, make sure you're doing your due diligence before bringing them a potential deal so they begin to build trust in you.

Follow-up is a big part of the 80/20 rule. You need to do whatever you can to firmly plant yourself in the 20% category, and thorough follow-up is one way to do that. You're doing things that other investors won't do, and that will make you stand apart (**Bedgoodism #12: Hold Yourself Accountable, No One Else Will**). You will gain a reputation of being a performer, someone who can get things done. That will build confidence, and investors love to work with confident people. There's too much at risk in investing to deal with people you're unsure of. Building your reputation right from the start will get you far, and consistent, thorough follow up is one way to do that. Take a look at the case study on the next page for an example of how I've used follow-up to get more deals in my own business.

Case Study #5: Good Follow-Up Will Get You Paid Every Time (Mandy Lane)

Mandy Lane was brought to me by a birddog who had become a wholesaler. He was very experienced and knew what to look for when wholesaling houses. He had also dabbled in flipping, but his business model didn't include flipping houses with cracked slabs or foundation issues; he didn't want the headache or liability. But here is what's funny. I had seen Mandy Lane when it was on the MLS and on the open market before he had it under contract. I had made an offer with the listing agent, but the bank did not accept my offer. My follow-up was a little lacking at the time because I was flipping houses and not doing much wholesaling. But this guy's follow-up was great, which is why he was able to get this house.

He kept making offers. He got contractor bids and submitted them with his offers. He kept getting rejected. Months and months went by, and this house just sat. Why? The bank wasn't lowering their price enough to get people to take the risk on the house. Banks will lower the price a little every month. Asset managers can't see how bad the house is because they often live in another state and work strictly through emails and phone calls. This wholesaler kept following up, and eventually the bank gave in… to whom? To this one guy who had been hounding them for months and months.

What can you learn from this? When birddogging and wholesaling, do what others aren't doing, follow up! Track all your offers. Either have an assistant or VA (virtual assistant) do it, or if you are just starting out, you do it. Diligent follow-up can literally get you 10 more deals a year. This wholesaler called me off of a bandit sign, asking if I was looking for deals. I said yes, and he told me about the property on Mandy Lane. I said, "No thanks, I've already seen that one. The bank is crazy." He told me he had it tied up and could sell it to me at "this price." I was shocked and asked how he got them to agree to such a low price. He said he submitted contractor bids over and over again and kept making offers every couple weeks. I told him his price to me was high, but that I would go look at the house again and make a final decision.

Mandy Lane was a cracked slab house – literally cracked in half. It was one of the worst I had seen, especially once I really started looking at it. Overall, the house was in pretty good shape and would be a simple remodel of the kitchen, bathrooms, new carpet, and paint. But the foundation was the kicker. It was a single story, 3 bed, 2 bath with two large living rooms and a huge laundry room in the middle of the house, with additional hook-ups in the garage. The house was sitting on a slope, which was half fill dirt and half solid dirt. The half of the house that was on the fill had literally dropped 12 inches and would have to be raised up. The drop was affecting the roof, the structure, and the foundation. Half the house was slowly sliding down a hill. This was *not* going to be a cheap project. But the house had a lot going for it. It was in a quiet neighborhood, was a single story, and had lots of space, large rooms, and vaulted ceilings. But it wasn't enough to get the value up to what I needed. I needed to figure out a way to increase the value of this home if I was going to be able to fix the slab and make a profit.

I walked the property for about an hour. In my head I moved walls around, moved the kitchen, doorways, and windows. I tried to find a way to add value. Then it came to me, add a junior master bedroom, which is a smaller bedroom with its own private bathroom. It's great for families with a teenager or college-age son or daughter, or it's great for people who have an elderly parent who needs to live with them. This house was huge, and it had two living rooms. It really only needed one. Plus it had a huge laundry room, but the attached garage had additional plumbing hook-ups. I decided to build walls and convert that living room into a large bedroom and turn the laundry room into a private bathroom. That was my added value I needed to bring my price up. There's one last thing. The comps in the neighborhood were barely scraping what I would need to sell for to make a profit. So I drove my comps. As I was driving on the same street I saw a house with a For Sale sign that I had seen as *Pending* on the MLS (it was not sold yet, so we didn't know what it was going to sell for).

A man was pulling in the driveway, so as any good investor does, I talked to their neighbors and gathered intel. I asked, "How are you? Nice house. What's it selling for?" He said, "Oh, we are supposed to close tomorrow, and it will be sold for $455,000." I almost couldn't believe what he said. This was a 4 bed, 3 bath, just like I was going to make my house. The 3 bed, 2 baths were only selling for around $400,000. My wholesaler did not have the vision to turn it into a four bedroom. He did not have the crews to tackle foundation issues, and he didn't have the knowledge that a house four doors away from his was going to sell for $455,000 the next day!

I immediately called the wholesaler and asked him if he could lower his price any more. Why not ask, right? I'm always negotiating. He said "No, as a matter of fact another guy has said he will buy it from me and is going to meet me this afternoon with a $10,000 non-refundable check and buy it from me. But, since I offered it to you first and since I want to do a deal with you, if you can get me a check for $10,000, promise you can close in 10 days, and sign a contract in the next few hours, I will give it to you." I said, "Yes, no problem." Then I thought to myself, "OMG! I don't have $10,000. I can't close in 10 days."

I reminded myself that this was a deal. I had to perform. I had to find the money. *"Find the deal, and the money will find you. Ok, so let's get on the phone and find the money."* I made three phone calls. The first investor I called came and looked at the property immediately. Then he went with me to meet the wholesaler, and he wrote him a $10,000 check and signed the contract. I made a side deal with him for a profit split and that was it. I had found another property, bought it with someone else's money because I had vision, and brought a deal to the table to a hungry investor. The wholesaler and I were both making offers on the same property, but he got it because his follow-up was better than mine. Because of my relationship and networking, he trusted me and brought me the deal.

In the end he made money, I made money, and my investor partner made money. We all won. New relationships were born, and I'm still buying wholesales and selling him wholesales to this day!

Finding Buyers

Before you do anything – as you're finishing up your rehab, post a sign in the yard saying, "Coming Soon" and "For Sale" to start attracting attention.

Trying to find the right buyer for your house can be a time killer (**Bedgoodism #6: Measure Your R.O.T.: Return On Time**). Depending on your exit strategy, there are some things you can do to find buyers without sacrificing your valuable time. If you are wholesaling to another investor, the best thing you can do is ensure you have a diverse list of investors because they are buyers. We talked about this earlier – the more you network at seminars, boot camps, workshops, and REIA meetings, the more types of investors and cash buyers you will meet. Be sure to introduce yourself (**Bedgoodism #5: Networking & Face Time**) and collect their business cards. Then add those names on your buyer's list so that when you come across a great deal, you'll be able to reach out to the right investor to move the property.

Another way to find buyers as a wholesaler is through Facebook. This is a strategy I've used and still use. Build your network on Facebook, and let people know what you're doing.

When you have a deal and don't have a buyer right away, post the details on your Facebook page (or to any groups you belong to) to extend your reach.

Yet another great source is Craigslist, which is completely free. Craigslist is great for posting properties for sale. Investors will contact you, and you can continue to grow your buyers list. Real estate brokers are on Craigslist searching for potential listings and scouring the market for homes their buyers want that may not be listed. While you are there, take some time after you post your ad to look at others because you just may find your next deal. Keep your postings short, sweet, and engaging. Humorous titles catch people's attention, such as "3/2/2 with Man cave" or "Mailbox for sale, comes with Free 3/2 House." Describe the property like a homeowner would, and ask that people who are interested call you or email you with their name, best number, and best time to call.

If you're a rehabber creating homes you intend to sell to retail buyers (people who plan to live in it themselves, not investors) and are ready to find the perfect buyer for your newly remodeled house, make sure the first thing you do is get it MLS-ready. The MLS is so powerful and allows you to reach the greatest amount of buyers without a lot of out-of-pocket expense. Once your rehab is complete, have professional photographs taken of the house (don't compromise quality by relying on ones you take with your smartphone) to use in your MLS listing. Professional photos with proper lighting are a must and will pay for themselves with higher offers. Your rehab photos should look like a bright, beautiful, glitzy hotel room at the Ritz, not like a dingy Motel 6!

A word of caution to new rehabbers: I emphasize NEW rehabbers, first timers. Don't be tempted to list your house as a *For Sale By Owner* (FSBO) to save the money of hiring a real estate broker. Take advantage of the broker's network and their buyers list. The money you will pay in commission to a good, hard-working real estate broker will be well worth it.

If you do happen to have your real estate license, I don't recommend listing your own properties. It is best to give the listing to someone else and pay him or her a flat fee or discounted commission to do it. This way a third party has handled all the paperwork, not you. You need to be cautious with the paperwork involved; there is a risk of mismanagement or error, especially if you are dealing with a lot of properties. If you still want to list your own (and go against my advice), make sure you're carrying E & O insurance to guard against any errors or omissions on the paperwork.

There are some of you who will be in markets where the best type of exit strategy is to create rental grade homes that you sell to investors for buy and hold purposes. It is critical to build a cash buyer list, a list of investors who buy for cash. You can then save on real estate broker commissions by selling your home to cash buyers. These kinds of houses also traditionally take less time to sell and definitely take less time to close, since you're not waiting 30+ days for financing. Again, your market, network, and personal risk tolerance will mold the kind of real estate investing you focus on.

Let real estate brokers list your properties for you (preferably an investor-friendly broker). Take advantage of their reach, their marketing, and their buyers list. A good real estate agent angel is all you need for buying *and* selling. The bottom line is this: *if you're trying to find your own buyers by listing it as a FSBO to save a little money on the commission, then you're definitely wasting time and not finding MORE leads to turn into deals.*

Understanding the Paperwork

Depending on the deal type, MLS, HUD, Fannie Mae (on market), or non-MLS (off market), there may be a lot of paperwork involved with any real estate investing transaction. As you work your way through the stages of being an investor, the amount of paperwork will increase. When you're just starting out as a birddog, there is not much paperwork at all. It may be something as simple as a written contract with the investor you're giving the lead to, outlining your birddog fee. But as you begin to wholesale and then progress to rehabbing and you're dealing with banks, contractors, buyers, and sellers, the amount of paperwork involved increases. There are professional TC's (Transaction Coordinators) out there who can handle your paperwork for you, too.

If you're following my advice to this point, you've started to build your network and are regularly attending seminars and REIA club meetings. Hopefully you've even identified a mentor. And this is how you'll get to learn about all the paperwork involved. It will be through discussions, listening, learning, and then actually doing that you'll learn how to navigate. Never hesitate to ask your mentor when you're unsure.

If you've chosen a mentor who is open to sharing and guiding you, he or she will be able to point you in the right direction.

Below is a list of the most common paperwork involved in a transaction:

⇒ Residential purchase agreement (Offer).

⇒ Proof of funds.

⇒ Deposit check.

⇒ Preliminary title.

⇒ Transfer disclosures.

⇒ Escrow instructions.

⇒ Loan documents.

⇒ Termite reports.

⇒ Home inspection reports.

⇒ Appraisals.

⇒ Permits.

⇒ Contracts with contractors.

⇒ Material purchase receipts.

⇒ Invoices from contractors.

⇒ Bookkeeping paperwork.

The more experienced you become and the more deals you're involved in, the more familiar you will be with the paperwork. *Note*: Most real estate brokers have a TC or Transaction Coordinator to help you with paperwork during a purchase and re-sale. If they don't, ask them why.

Now that all of the marketing is done, the deals have flowed through your pipeline, and the paperwork is buttoned up, it's time to enjoy my favorite part of real estate investing, the story behind each deal. The rest of the book is dedicated to bringing the stories you saw on A&E's *Flipping San Diego* to life and filling in the blanks, from how we got the deals to how we fared financially. I saved them for the end because now you will better understand the work and lessons behind the scenes.

So grab a cup of coffee or tea (or your favorite adult beverage), and settle in for some great stories!

Behind the Scenes of *Flipping San Diego*

——•◆•——

How *Flipping San Diego* Came to Be

Flipping San Diego was almost a right time, right place, right people situation. It's a great example of where networking, face time, and telling people what you do for a living all came together; everything lined up.

But how did doing what I love result in a TV show?

I've told you how important it is to always be networking and telling people what you're doing. I was still working as a real estate agent and going to investing seminars to meet other investors. My goal was to meet other investors and birddog for them to learn about wholesaling. I wanted to create opportunities to flip houses without using my own money. I was learning about wholesaling while still driving buyers around town. I was doing everything I could to learn and grow. When I was working on my sixth flip, I was actively posting what I was doing on Facebook, letting everyone know. I would email my finished property listings and pictures from the MLS to real estate brokers and agents. My broker took notice of all this activity. At the time he was the president-elect of the San Diego Association of Realtors. He sent me a message explaining that he received an email from a TV producer looking for real estate flippers for a TV show, and here was the link to an application. I got his message but didn't do anything about it because it seemed like a waste of time. But, I did keep the link. Honestly, I didn't feel worthy of sending in an application for a TV show about flipping houses. I'm sure they wanted someone "other than me," right? Someone with more experience or a better "story." Essentially, I talked myself out of doing anything about it and going to the next step.

Even though the producers didn't know what I was actually doing, meaning what level of flipping I was doing, I talked myself out of it by figuring they wouldn't want me because they were probably looking for a big company doing lots of deals. I still didn't do anything about it. One day my girl-friend said to me, "What do you have to lose? You don't know what they're looking for; you don't know what they want un-til you try, so why not fill it out?" After I thought about it, she was right. She believed in me. Why didn't I?? Nothing to lose, right? (**Bedgoodism #14: Find People Who Believe In You... And Leave The Others Behind**) Why wouldn't I see where this goes? "Luck" as some would call it, or an "opportunity" as I would call it, had just dropped in my lap. Why not go for it? At least I wouldn't look back one day and say, *"Damn, look at that.* Flipping San Diego *is on the air and I could have tried out for that show! That could have been ME!"* But I was hesitant to fill out the application as a solo investor because I wanted to hedge my bets. If I was going to go for it, I wanted to go big time. Go big, or go home.

I did some research and noticed that most other flipping shows seemed to have a partnership or a team of characters. I asked myself, whom could I bring in for this? Chief Denney's name came to mind. I had worked with him already on a number of projects, and we had a great relationship and talked all the time about deals, but mainly we believed in each other. He was a friend, mentor, and full-time investor. I called him up and told him about the opportunity. I said, "Hey man, maybe we can have some fun, and what have we got to lose?" Of course in Chief Denney style he said, "Sure, why not?" We completed the application, submitted it, and actually got a re-ply! Hmm. That's interesting. Okay, now what?

Now they wanted a 5-minute video so they could see our personalities and character in our business. If you've ever filmed a video, you know that five minutes can go VERY fast, especially when you are trying to show your personalities while getting your point across. We got together and put our "What do you think TV producers whom we've never met would like to see about two dorks who flip houses in San Diego?" hats. Because Chief and I are both outside-the-box thinkers and are very comfortable living outside our comfort zone, we knew we had to do that little extra that other people trying out might not do. We went for it like we always did and made an investment. If we were going to roll the dice, we were going to go big time.

We hired an acquaintance of Chief's who was a professional videographer and editor who had worked on reality shows, and then we got our crew together, different characters that were involved in our rehabs. At first we did some of our own filming with our smart phones, and then the videographer filmed some of the more dramatic footage with a professional camera. All of the production was filmed at actual rehab houses that we owned. We tried to guess what the producers might want so we filmed real-life examples of what we were doing, then filmed some drama that was happening with the houses and our contractors, and then we created a little extra drama to show the producers we had some personality. Then we had the videographer edit everything together with music, graphics, and of course before and afters of the projects. All of this cost us a couple thousand dollars and our time.

To our surprise, we received word that we were one of the favorites – a top contender – and that the next step was that they were going to send one of their professional TV videographers to shoot some footage! Plus we found out that the production company, Departure Films, was the same company that had produced *Flip This House*, which was a hugely popular show. Yeah, right? But they never sent out a videographer. We were told someone else had been chosen and that no more interviews would take place. It was over. But at least we tried. And it felt good to have been a top contender. We had done what others wouldn't do and put our best foot forward. We tried to take an opportunity and take it as far as we could, like any good entrepreneur would do. We felt good about that and went back to flipping houses. We didn't expect to hear from them again, but a year later, we did.

At that time, another flipping show was just airing on TV. It's then that we got a call, finally. They wanted us to try out again. This time, just Chief and me. No other characters for now. We hired the same videographer and made another 5-minute video to send in. We came up with new properties, new drama, and new scenarios. Again they loved it, and this time sent out their own videographer. Between us we had several houses, and all were in different stages of rehabbing so we had perfect opportunities to get some great footage. We really wanted to impress the videographer and have the best chance of succeeding. The timing seemed to be right. About a month later we got news that the A&E Network had funded the project and sent over the contracts to us, and *Flipping San Diego* was underway!

We learned as we went along. We filmed hundreds of hours for each house that the editors then pieced together for a one-hour finished episode. There are only so many storylines that could fit into each episode, but the film crew was there to capture it all, and then some! Doing the show was draining at times, frustrating at times, but all in all fun and exciting. It was surreal in the beginning, but it was all worth it; it was really cool in the end to see it all done and to watch the episodes on my own TV screen. As a reality TV junkie, it was pretty cool to see my own name for the first time in the TV guide.

Really it all started with an email that someone sent to me because they knew what I was doing and they believed in me. **Bedgoodism #3: Make Your Own Luck**. I always strive to make my own luck. Control my own destiny. You have to be prepared to take advantage of opportunities when they present themselves. If an opportunity seems to be too hard or too tough, take a step back and ask yourself, "What will happen if I do this? What will happen if I don't do this? Will I have regrets? Is my competitor going to do this?"

I have had so many walls put up in front of me, I don't even know how not to take the extra step to make things happen. This was just another example of how I've always done things. Come on, who would have thought I would be starring in a franchised television show? I picked up an opportunity and ran with it. Set your own goals high. Who knows what will happen when you do?

Acquisitions: How We "Got" the Houses on *Flipping San Diego*

The Real Story Behind the Scenes

You've seen what I do on the show, but do you ever wonder how these houses were found? People always want to know whether the producers brought us the houses or if we had to find the houses for the show. The short answer is we had to find the houses; we had to bring the houses to the show. The producers and the network wanted real, legitimate flippers; we had to prove that we were legitimate and could perform. Do you wonder why someone would be willing to sell their house rather than fix it up themselves and make the money? Or for that matter, why someone else didn't buy the property before me?

Flipping San Diego focuses on a very small part of the deal cycle, the "fix it up and sell it" part. Almost anyone can fix up a house, just call a contractor, maybe a designer, dump some money into it, pray for no surprises, survive the drama, finish the project, call a real estate broker, and sell the house. Hopefully for a profit. Simple, right? Not so fast. The producers had to approve the houses we used. They had to agree that it would be a "good" one to use. We had to give them an idea of what we were going to do for the rehab. They didn't want to know how we got the houses; they wanted the before and after and the in-between.

Well, the real magic happens during the searching and in turn the *acquisition* phase. The turning a "lead into a deal" phase.

If we didn't get a house, we didn't have a show. In real estate you will hear, "you make your money when you BUY the house," meaning if you buy it right, did your due diligence, and gave yourself a cushion, you shouldn't lose money no matter what happens! How did we actually acquire the houses we featured in the show? Why did we choose that particular house? How does it seem we keep getting "lucky" with great houses? How did we have time to find these houses?

Let's take a look at the houses we featured on **Flipping San Diego** *and I'll explain how we got each one.*

#1: "House of Horrors"

"Guys, there's a secret compartment under the garage floor... and there's something in it!"

Located in Allied Gardens, this house was filled to the brim with the seller's belongings before we bought it or even saw it. The seller had moved out long ago and was now just using the property for storage. We would soon find out that one of the things still there were the ashes of her late husband! Don't worry, if you didn't see the episode, we tracked down the seller and returned her husband to her, and she was extremely grateful. She kept his ashes in the garage because that's where he most loved to spend time, so it was sort of a tribute to him. And YES, that was the REAL previous owner on the show, a very sweet lady indeed.

- ⇒ Purchased for **$371,000**.
- ⇒ **$50,000** rehab budget.
- ⇒ **$56,000** actual rehab cost.
- ⇒ Listed for **$540,000** value range.
- ⇒ Sold for **$540,000**.
- ⇒ **Total profit $79,000**.

When we found this house, we had just started setting up for filming so we were actually looking for a house that we could use for the show; we needed a good one. I got an email from our acquisitions team telling me about a lead that they thought was a good deal. I ran the numbers to see what kind of deal it really was. This was on a Sunday afternoon, and I remember thinking, I can just ignore this lead and keep watching the football games – both of my favorite teams were playing – so this lead can wait, or I can look within myself, do what others are unwilling to do on a Sunday, and record the games and watch them later. I knew I needed a house, especially for the show, and the competition from other investors was fierce. Hopefully all my competitors would stay home and watch the game, or they were all at the beach!

I thought, "What am I going to do to forward my business and do what everyone else is doing? Or not doing? Am I going to take one more step and do what everyone else is not doing?" It really was an internal struggle that I had. I was burned out from the week and wanted some down time, but I knew I needed to explore this lead. My business revolves around finding deals and beating others to the punch. I contemplated this lead and found out more information about it. It was a fairly new listing, 1,800 sq. ft., but only 2 beds, 2 baths. With that square footage, I knew I could move some walls around, so I looked up comps that were 4 beds, 2 or 3 baths. I always look for houses that I can add value to. It's called "vision." The seller and the broker often don't have a vision to see the changes that I can see, so they will price a house low. If you have a vision, you'll set yourself apart – think outside the box or as I like to say in house flipping, think INSIDE the box. Don't just look at the numbers because those can change significantly if you can change the house and make it better. That's what I saw in this house – I saw pictures on the MLS, knew the bed and bath count, and knew I could modify it without much trouble since the square footage was 1,800.

I DVR'd the football game, changed into presentable clothes, got in my car, and drove over to the house about 20 minutes away. There were other investors and looky-loos there. One guy, though, appeared to be locking up the house. He asked me if he could help me. I said, "No thanks, I'm an investor, just here to look at the house and make an offer." His eyes lit up, and his voice seemed to reflect interest, which surprised me for a second because I thought he was a real estate broker showing the house to his clients. But he turned out to be the listing agent! Score! Everyone else had left by this point; my timing was good. I was able to bond with the listing agent, *and* I was able to do a full inspection on the house right in front of him. *(Tip:* When the broker is at the house, I make sure he sees me fully inspect the house – a lot of investors will do the opposite by acting cool and not looking at the house at all. I inspect the foundation, roofs, etc., plus ask a lot of questions and let him know I can handle anything. This helps him remember ME over other investors when he sees my offer later on. The listing agent's guidance is what influences which offer the seller will take, so every little bit counts when there is a lot of competition for deals.)

I explained that I would go back to my office, run my comps, present my offer, and would close quickly if I could get the property for the right price. I also mentioned he could write my offer (be my agent) plus I would relist it with him if the numbers worked. I knew he was in the business to get the right price, best terms, and best buyer for his seller – I had that dialogue with him, so we knew what we were getting into and had an understanding about each other up front.

To me this is further bonding and trust building, key to relationship building. He decided to write my offer and represent me. I made an offer I felt comfortable with. I didn't write my highest and best upfront but one that got me into the mix. I prepared for the counter offer. If you get some intel from the agent that there will be a multiple counter offer, leave yourself room to come up with your offer and still be comfortable. All the stars were aligning, but it was not easy. The broker said he knew I did my inspections; "I've met you and know you'll perform. Your offer is not the highest, but my seller needs to sell and I feel you will perform." "The seller has five or six offers, and you need to be in this range to be competitive; then it is up to the seller to choose," he said. The broker is required to present all offers he receives to the buyer; it is a fiduciary duty that all real estate brokers have to their sellers. I *then* gave my **highest and best** offer (meaning price and terms). I sent my offer over. There was another, higher offer, but he was not convinced about that one. I made a strong offer, was able to put down a large deposit and offer a zero-day inspection contingency so I could get *my* offer accepted on *my* terms

Tip: A zero-day inspection contingency doesn't scare me if I've seen the house, but your contractor or money partner hasn't yet – don't sweat it – make the offer. It can take 3-10 days for a seller to review offers, make a decision on what to do or to accept the offer. Inspect the property while you're waiting, during that window of time IF you think you might get the deal. The paperwork will take a few days, so get your contractor over there. Once there is a fully executed contract (signed by all parties), you open escrow and a contract will not be fully binding until money has changed hands (deposit received by escrow).

The broker was comfortable with my offer. He saw and recognized that I went one step beyond what others were doing. He knew I was the right buyer. Plus it was a bonus that I was the guy with the cash, not just an acquisitions person representing someone else who hadn't even seen the house yet. I was not the highest priced offer, but I was the best overall offer. My offer was officially accepted five days later. This broker ended up getting three commissions on that house, meaning he "triple ended it" and gave me a discount when he resold it for me because of that.

Tip when listing with a broker: When I relist with an agent, I offer them a commission based on the sale price, not just a flat commission for "any" sales price. I start them at the low end of the commission scale if the house sells at the bottom of my range. This seems to give them more incentive to work a little harder to get me a higher price. Plus we have an understanding in writing of what compensation they can expect to have. It also shows them that if I make extra money, I am willing to share the wealth, and this helps keep my relationships strong.

Here's a bonus Bedgoodism: Sharing The Wealth Has Made Me Wealthy.

I know how important a commission is for real estate brokers, and honestly, they're the best birddogs out there! According to the RESPA rules – Real Estate Settlement Procedures Act – I am not allowed to cut a check to a real estate agent; it's unethical because I am not their broker; a licensed broker must pay real estate agents/Realtors. I can, however, give a documented increased commission on the HUD through escrow; it's not hidden. When I do that, escrow writes a check to the agent's broker, who pays the agent. This little bonus makes the agent happy, and hopefully he or she will look for more deals for me. Win - win! This house was all about me getting up off my couch on a Sunday afternoon to make things happen, doing that one thing that other people won't do.

#2: "Critter House" (also known as the "Caddy Shack" episode)

"That thing is the size of a cat!"

Located in Lakeside, a rural suburb of San Diego, this house was filled with problems and surprises, mostly of the rodent-variety. We also had to deal with permitting problems, which resulted in a stop work order, but we didn't let that stop us! For this house, it was all about *"Gophers and rats and inspectors, oh my!"*

⇒ Purchase price **$170,000.**

⇒ **$45,000** rehab budget.

⇒ **$227,000** total investment.

⇒ Listed for **$305,000.**

⇒ Sold for **$320,000.**

⇒ **Total profit $73,000.**

This was another house that was listed by a real estate agent who brings me a lot of my deals, Alicia (my real estate angel). This was a pre-MLS/pocket listing (***Tip***: If you find an REO or short sale agent, they will be able to let you see a house and run an inspection before it goes on the MLS. This puts you at the front of the pack, and every little edge counts). I gave my agent my offer price, so when the house hits the market, my offer goes in immediately. Is this considered cheating? No, it goes on with every broker who is a listing agent – it is part of the business. Remember, real estate brokers are in the business of selling property fast. So showing it before it hits the

MLS is legal and encouraged; a broker will try to show the house to as many performers as possible to sell the property.

Because of my good relationship with the agent, I was able to find out about the property before it went on the MLS and make an offer the minute it hit the market. The asset manager took my offer despite multiple offers being submitted on this property – it was the *best* offer he received on the property. Remember, offers aren't just about the best or highest price, but are about the entire offer and includes the terms, which are the deposit, the length of escrow, and how the property will be funded (with cash or a loan, etc.).

Find your own real estate agent angel – one who will feed you properties for a long time. The best place to meet such a real estate agent is at a property – where they are working. Go to an open house and begin to build a rapport. Ask them about the property and about their business. Remember, you want to be the first one they think of when a property be-comes available. Then follow up with them continuously to see if they have new listings coming up.

#3: "Crack House"

"Eventually we had to tear down the front of the house."

This house is located in La Mesa and came with a lot of problems. The house was sitting on a hillside, and it needed work to bring it up to the neighborhood standard. The garage was actually sitting on the hill, which was fill dirt.

⇒ Purchased for **$280,000**.

⇒ **$55,000** rehab budget.

⇒ **$378,000** total investment.

⇒ Listed for **$540,000**.

⇒ Sold for **$535,000** *cash.*

⇒ **Total profit $118,000.**

Alicia, my real estate agent angel, found this property for me. I knew there were a lot of problems with it, and we tried to anticipate as much as possible as we got into the rehab. But as often happens, there ended up being a lot more problems. The house was difficult to acquire. I was making multiple offers on it before we even started filming anything for the show. Other potential buyers would go into escrow on the house, get the inspection, and then cancel. After the third or fourth time this happened, three months had gone by. I kept checking on the house. Ok, I was watching it like a hawk (follow up!).

I make it a habit of keeping a watchful eye on these types of properties because I know they can fall out of escrow. When I do this, I get at least five more deals a year from properties that have fallen out of escrow, and I buy them. Once again, it's that extra thing that I will do that gets me a few more deals a year. I continue to bond with the agent and check in on the sale of the house. Once it goes into *Pending* status on the MLS, most investors forget about it. I don't. Every once in a while you'll get one this way. There were "false investors" making offers, someone who would make an offer to tie it up while they looked for an investor to bring into the deal. The broker knew I was a performer (remember, I had worked with this agent before and had kept following up on this property). The asset manager asked who was a performer and the broker said that I was. They ended up dropping the price of the house and accepting my offer, just to get it off their books and out of their hair. **Failure + Persistence = Success**

During that time (2 to 3 month span), the value of the house was actually going up. Remember, I'm tracking the house while other offers are happening. I'm also continuing to bond with the real estate agent. The value of the house increased, but the asset manager dropped the price because he was frustrated. I stuck to my guns and didn't raise my purchase price because I knew the property was going to be a nightmare.

Once we finally got the rehab underway, we found problem after problem. The rehab went way over budget, but we still made a very good profit on the house. We did have to spend money to make money – we reconfigured an unused living room into a fourth bedroom, installed a new kitchen, did brand new landscaping – all to further increase the value of the house. It was the perfect storm; it was a red flag house; it had everything going wrong, but everything going right once we fixed it. It had views and was in a desirable area, near the trolley with access to the highway and shopping. I knew the location would overcome everything, and it did.

#4: "Tiny Tiny House"

"We took a tiny, tiny house and turned it into a tiny house."

This house is located in the North Park neighborhood of San Diego, and it really was tiny – just 530 sq. ft. "It's a Lego house."

⇒ Purchased for **$249,000**.

⇒ **$47,000** rehab budget.

⇒ **$317,000** total investment ($21,000 over budget).

⇒ Listed and sold for **$450,000**.

⇒ **Total profit $94,000.**

Chief brought us this house through our acquisitions team – the numbers looked ok, but the property was *so* small and on a busy street, but in a great location otherwise. It was just two blocks away from a real up-and-coming area. Chief and I knew the listing broker but hadn't done a deal with him in a while. There had already been offers made on this house, but then they were falling out of escrow. The bank was not budging on their price. So as not to risk losing the deal, Chief took this house over from the acquisitions team, and he bonded with the broker. He explained that we wanted the house, "but it's so small, there's a lot we have to do to it to make it livable again. Blah, blah, blah..."

Chief made an offer that worked, and they accepted it. By this point, the bank was done with this house. They wanted it out of their inventory and out of their hair. Cha-CHING! Chief and I talked it over and even considered cancelling, but decided we could make it work because the location was amazing and the market was creeping up a bit in value in this particular area. We had a vision for this house. We hate to pass on deals, especially ones that get our creative minds working. Despite running into significant problems and my feelings that the house was too tiny, even for an Oompa-Loompa, I'm glad Chief stuck to his guns and we went with our gut instinct on this one because the finished product was amazing. Someone found their dream home, and we walked away with a significant profit.

Tip: You will run into real estate agents but not actually be able to do deals with them at that time. It is to your benefit to continue bonding with them and following up with them.

#5: "Double Trouble"

"This is not an easy business – to succeed, you don't worry about the why, just find the house that someone wants to get rid of and worry about the how."

I had made an offer on this property before we knew we were going to be filmed for TV. Chief didn't even know about it for many months because it was in short sale negotiations with the bank. It was just one of several I had working in my pipeline of potential deals. Located in a diverse area of San Diego called Normal Heights, this was a two-unit property that had two detached houses on one lot, so for the show we set up a sort of rehabbing competition between Chief and me. For this one, I think the story behind the acquisition of this house is more interesting than the actual rehab. Do you have your coffee ready? Check this out:

- ⇒ Purchase price **$320,000**.
- ⇒ **$96,000** rehab budget for two houses.
- ⇒ **17,000** over budget.
- ⇒ **$514,000** total investment.
- ⇒ Listed for **$575,000**.
- ⇒ Sold for **$680,000** (*BIDDING WAR!*).
- ⇒ **Total profit $166,000.**

A tenant was living in the front house, and the owner of both houses was living in the back house. Both houses were part of one parcel, and it was going into foreclosure. The houses were a shambles, but when I see that, I see dollar signs! The house was a no brainer for any investor. The key to this deal was my mindset – I had to chase, network, and build relationships. The house could not be sold due to a clouded title. The real estate broker for the properties called me and asked if I would want to make an offer and of course I said, "Yes!" I like a challenge. The reason no one had bought the houses yet is because the owner of the property, who was living in the back house, promised or implied that he would sell the front house to the tenant for $35,000. The tenant paid him, but neither one of them apparently put that deal on paper, and if they did, it was never recorded at the city. It was all verbal, he said/she said. The owner began having financial problems and was losing everything, and the entire property (both houses) was now in pre-foreclosure.

The tenant, living in the front house, would not leave because he felt like an owner, especially since he had paid $35,000 for it (supposedly). Even though the house was worth 10 times that amount. The tenant (wisely) hired an attorney who clouded the title with a "lis pendens" (a written notice that a lawsuit has been filed concerning the house involving either the title of the property or the claimed ownership interest in it). The tenant was living in the house for free at this point and had been for over a year apparently, not paying the owner's mortgage or paying rent.

Since the property was still in pre-foreclosure I had an opportunity to buy it as a short sale if the owner/seller would accept an offer. I thought, "Hmm, let me make a low offer to the seller, but give room for the bank who owns the mortgage to come up when they counter me," which I most certainly assumed they would. The occupants had reasons for selling the house; they wanted to get rid of it, and I wanted to be the one they sold it to. It was my job to convince them that my offer would be the best. Let me say one thing here. For anyone thinking I'm greedy and don't care about the seller, and that all I care about is money, please remember, this family was in dire straits. The bank was going to take the house from them, call the Sheriff, have them booted out, and then sell the property anyway. So I found a solution to keep this from happening AND help the seller and tenant, which the bank certainly didn't care about! Read on please...

The owner finally agreed to my low offer. He didn't care about my low offer because it was a short sale and it was up to the lien holder or bank to decide what was a fair price at this point. He wouldn't receive any money from the bank anyway. (**Note**: Every state has different rules and laws regarding buying pre-foreclosures and especially falsifying documents or defrauding a seller or a bank. Take this part of investing seriously and cross all your T's and dot your I's. Consult an attorney and real estate brokers when doing these transactions. If you do it right, short sales can be very lucrative and can help out the seller and even the bank). It took three months for the bank to get back with me (August to October), but the bank accepted my low offer! They didn't even counter. I was happily surprised. The title, however, was still clouded because of the lis pendens, and this was why I was getting such a smokin' deal. During this time, I tried to get a hold of the tenant's attorney. I offered cash for keys, trying to give the tenant money to walk away so I could get the lis pendens removed and close escrow. The answer was always the same, "Talk to my attorney." So I did. The attorney wanted to hold out for more money even while my real estate agent was trying to show them the benefits of accepting my offer. The lis pendens remained.

Alicia (my "real estate agent angel" who also brought me this deal) was able to delay the trustee sale by 30 days the first time, and then delayed it another 30 days a second time. If the house went to trustee sale, that meant it might go to public auction at the courthouse steps. I knew that if that happened, someone else would buy it, and I'd lose the deal. Why wouldn't I go through everything to get this deal done like any other investor would do? It had the potential for a big profit. I was completely frustrated and knew I had to start thinking bigger, but honestly, I was beginning to lose hope. In December, I still could not get a hold of the attorney, and the tenant was not talking to anyone anymore. What was even more frustrating was that since I had made my initial offer almost five months earlier, values for this type of property had begun to skyrocket. The numbers were so phenomenal that it seemed too good to be true.

I was stumped. I really needed to make this work. I refocused and decided to give it another shot. There had to be a way. I couldn't let this go to auction and see some other investor make a mint on it. I had control of this property with an accepted offer from the bank, and I had to keep that control as long as possible, at all costs.

Two days before the final trustee sale, I literally woke up that morning thinking about the house. I'm pretty sure I had been dreaming about it (and NOT in a good way). Alicia texted me to say that the bank would not push back the trustee sale AGAIN. No more delays. I either had to have a letter from the attorney stating the lis pendens would be removed, or the house would go to auction and the bank would go to court with the attorney. I asked myself, "What was my only option? *To get the tenant and the attorney to sign a document releasing the lis pendens and delay the sale.*" In other words, I needed to make a deal and make it fast! This is the point where people either go to the next level or not. This is a life-changing deal – what would Trump do? What would Kyosaki do? What would I do? I had made my living making sure aircrafts did not drop out of the sky. Now I had to find a way to keep this deal from falling out of the sky! I had the mindset to dig another foot; the gold you're looking for might be right there, and you don't know it unless you keep digging. The worst thing is to find out another investor dug another foot and made the deal work when you could have just as easily gotten creative and made it work for you. If the house hasn't gone to the trustee sale yet, the deal is not done yet. There was still time for me to do something, anything I could.

So I put on a suit (I am a t-shirt and jeans kind of guy) and went to La Jolla to the attorney's office early in the morning. Up until this point he had ignored me or declined to meet with me. Once at the office, I introduced myself to the receptionist and told her that Mr. Attorney had asked me to meet him at his office (even though he had NOT). I further explained that I had never met him in person, and if she could please give me a nod when he came in the door. She agreed, not realizing I had just made her my accomplice. I waited and waited. Finally after several hours, an elderly gentleman in a suit walked in. The receptionist nodded at me and actually let the attorney know I was there to meet with him. Rather than waste too much time because I figured he was there for scheduled meetings with actual clients, I introduced myself as the man who was trying to purchase the duplex with the lis pendens. I said, "Mr. Attorney, the property is going to a trustee sale in less than 48 hours, and I'm here to make an offer and a solution to avoid a trustee sale. It's going to a trustee sale if we can't make a deal happen here today, and if that's the case, no one gets paid and your client could possibly end up on the street, and no one wants to see that happen, sir. He paused. Looked me up and down. Looked at the receptionist. And finally said, "My client is not interested. We think the bank will pay more than your offer." My heart sank. But I had come this far, so I said, "I get it. I understand. But if I can get a minute of your time, I'm here to ensure that your client gets some money because the bank might not offer him anything since there was no recorded agreement as to the sale of the property to your client." He paused, seemed to think for a second, and then to my surprise he asked me how much I was willing to offer. I knew the tenant had supposedly given $35,000 to the owner, but I was unwilling to pay that amount. But I was also unwilling to lose this property because I knew the value had risen significantly since I put it under contract. All of a sudden it was "go time." Put up or shut up. I started low. I said, "Sir I really feel that $12,000 is a fair offer, but, in the spirit of getting this deal done, I am willing to offer $15,000." The attorney looked at me for a split second and said, "No, I'm sure we can get more from the bank and that my client will not accept that amount." And he started to shuffle off.

I quickly let him know that he had really hit me hard with that "no," but I also asked him, "What would it take?" He paused. He was silent. I felt I was losing him! He could walk away at any second. I said, "Look, it's in everyone's benefit to get this deal done. I am **unwilling** to walk away from here without making a strong offer. I know that your client spent $35,000. Would you sign a piece of paper today that you will proceed to releasing the lis pendens and allowing this property to close with the current escrow if I offered your client $35,000?" Wow. Did I really just say that?? Gulp. After another pause, he looked at me and said, "Hmm, I think I can convince him to accept that." YES! I've made a deal. He said, "Get back with me in a couple of hours, send me an email, blah, blah blah." Yikes. We didn't have a couple of hours. So I explained that we didn't have two hours – the house would go to fore-closure if I didn't have a signed document right away to get over to the asset manager, who was in another time zone, pos-sibly Timbuktu, who would need time to accept, review, and then send to the bank's attorney for final review and lifting of the impending trustee sale date in 48 hours. That could take a day or so itself. So on a whim and with a little desperation in my voice, I said, "We could do an agreement right here, right now." I asked him if we could draft a handwritten agreement explaining the terms so that my agent would have something to email to the bank. He paused, and then said, "Sure, why not if you are willing to sign an agreement." So we wrote an agreement right then and there; the attorney actually told me what to write. I added some things to the agreement to protect both parties; we both signed it and agreed to talk later. I thanked the receptionist, and I was gone, smiling from ear-to-ear.

I immediately got on the phone with Alicia and told her the news. She was shocked and thankful. I had become her angel investor because I had just saved her commission! By that action, we were able to stop the trustee sale for the third time.

I didn't give away any money even though I offered more than I wanted to. I was focused on the urgency at hand, which was to get the required things in line and get the deal to the next step. As a real estate investor, you're the only one who cares about your success or failure – YOU are the one who has to get creative and make the deal happen. **Bedgoodism #3: Make Your Own Luck**. They stopped the trustee sale, and now we had to close by the end of the month, whether the tenant was still occupying the property or not!

I took Chief with me when I went back to see the attorney with a check for $35,000 and agreements for the tenant to leave within one month. The $35,000 would be put into the attorney's trust account, not the tenant's account, plus we agreed the tenant would be docked $1,000 off the $35,000 for each day after the close of escrow that they didn't leave. After 15 days he would not receive any of the $35,000. We had to make the penalty strong to motivate the tenant and his family to vacate the property.

The tenant ended up leaving two days late (with permission). And we paid the original seller $3,000 cash for keys to vacate the back house before the close of escrow in a separate agreement. In a bad situation, it became a win-win for all parties, including the bank. The tenant got paid. The seller got some money. The attorney got paid. The bank got paid. And of course Chief and I scored another stinky, smelly, money pit house. Yeah! That house was on my plate for many months in some form or fashion. This deal was about thinking differently and never giving up, and the result was one of my biggest profits on a deal ever. **Bedgoodism #16: Find A Way Around The Wall... Any Way.**

#6: "Cat Invasion"

Why would they come here and have a cat death party?"

Located in the City Heights area of San Diego.

⇒ Purchased for **$176,000.**

⇒ **$50,000** rehab budget.

⇒ **$51,000** actual rehab cost.

⇒ Sold for **$338,000.**

⇒ **Total profit $62,000.**

We had to act fast on this house. The deal made sense, the numbers made sense, and there was a very motivated seller. I knew the neighborhood pretty well, so I was eager to get a hold of this one. It isn't in a great area, but it is very close to an up-and-coming part of town called North Park, but the price points were better for first-time home buyers while still giving them access to North Park. Sometimes deals drop in your lap out of nowhere because you have networked yourself with other movers and shakers like acquisition teams, brokers, birddogs, and wholesalers. And you have to be able to act fast when these deals come available. This was one of those deals. We bought the house, showed it to the TV producers, and were promptly asked if we could hold it so they could film it for the show.

When the rehab first got underway, a real estate agent introduced a potential buyer to Chief. The agent allowed us to work directly with the potential buyer since we were so new into the project. This buyer was getting beat out on other houses, and she was a qualified buyer, so was getting frustrated. She actually came to see the property in the midst of the rehab (which was the source of some drama on the show). We eventually received top dollar for this house because Chief convinced us to cater to the potential buyer's home remodel requests, but also because we let her know the only way we would *not* put the finished product on the market once it was done was for her to make a very strong offer if the finished product was to her satisfaction. That would head off a potential bidding war. The only way for her to avoid that was to make an offer that we couldn't refuse. And she did! She was very aggressive with her offer contingent on the house appraising, which it did. It was risky to cater to one buyer because she had some very specific requests, but the gamble ended up paying off.

Even though we had a contingent offer about mid-way through the rehab, we did not actually have a written official offer until rehab was done to her satisfaction. As you can see by the show, when all was said and done, the buyer (and her entourage) was thrilled with the rehab and was excited to move into her first dream home.

Flipping San Diego Is Just One Chapter

———— ◆ ————

So much has happened in my life over the past year, the past five years, for that matter.

As a result of our TV show *Flipping San Diego*, I gained more exposure, which raised my credibility with my peers and real estate professionals in the industry, including brokers, lenders, other investors, etc. They continue to see me as a performer, and now they reach out more readily to do deals with me. It's a win-win all around and makes doing real estate deals even more exciting! It is opening doors in my networking world with people who are more established in all levels of business.

It's really had a snowball effect in my life; I've been able to experience exponential growth in opportunities, success, and development (remember **Bedgoodism #4: The Law of Exponentiality?**). My goal is to turn my success and exposure into business and personal growth ventures outside of real estate. Throughout my entire journey, I was (and still am) projecting what I want. Letting people know who I am and what

I do. Continuing to use face time to expose my dreams and passions to people who are more successful than I am. I was successful before the show and am now focusing on taking my business and life to the next level.

I'm living my life according to my **Bedgoodisms**, and creating new ones along the way. I have bigger goals in my life, and the show has allowed me to reach for them. I do have my own story, and I want to share that story with everyone I meet. I want to inspire others to go after their goals and their dreams and not let anything or anyone stand in their way. I want you to fight to find a way around, through, over, or under that wall.

Real estate investing has allowed me to enjoy life and live the life I want to live. I'm living out some of my own bucket list. It's allowed me to take my family on a last-minute cruise. I've rented two, 55-foot houseboats for a family vacation that was free for my family because I covered the costs. I've been able to get my dream car. I've been able to take off and go backpacking in many parts of the world. Being a successful real estate investor will allow me to live my ultimate dream of being a vagabond, an adventurer.

"Always be trying to live your bucket list or help someone else with his or her bucket list."

When I was just starting out, my goal was to earn enough money to visit my family in Georgia or maybe go to Las Vegas for the weekend. I accomplished that, and very quickly had to adjust my goals... upward! Real estate investing has allowed me to think much bigger; this business can change your life so quickly.

If you're not ready or willing to change your mindset, you'll be missing out on opportunities in real estate investing every day, and your dreams may just slip by, too. Just go out there and get started. Start small and think big, but START. Put your toe in the water before you immerse yourself, if you need to. It's OK! But take that first step to change your life, to build your own Rags to Riches journey.

To Learn More

For new Bedgoodisms, check out www.ChrisBedgood.com and follow me on Facebook at www.Facebook.com/ChrisBedgoodFlippingSanDiego.

Join my REIA: San Diego Real Estate Investors Association, at www.Facebook.com/SanDiegoREIA or www.SanDiegoREIA.com.

To learn more about my mentoring/coaching/education programs and how you can become a real estate veteran at my Real Estate Veteran Training Academy, visit www.REVtrainingacademy.com or www.VeteranFlipper.com.

Now It's Up to You

So now you're armed not only with information about getting on the road to your own Rags to Riches journey with your real estate investing business, but you have **my top Bedgood-isms (plus a bonus one!)** to help you stay motivated and keep pushing forward, no matter what.

What happens next is up to you. **Ask yourself...**

⇒ **How is your year going so far?**

⇒ **What specific things are you going to do to keep yourself motivated?**

⇒ **What changes are you going to make... starting right now?**

You *must* get outside of your comfort zone and do what others *won't* do if you want to go to the next level of success, and I can help take you there. Figure out what *you* want out of life. Write those goals down. Stick them on your mirrors and cupboards to remind you, and then *MAKE IT HAPPEN*!! No one cares about your success but **you**; it's up to **you** to make it happen.

What are you going to do *right now* to make your family's life better? Make a decision and then go for it. Don't let anyone or anything stop you... I didn't!

Do Something for a Veteran or Active Duty Member.

―――――◆―――――

It will make you feel amazing! Here are some suggestions of things you can do starting today:

1. Buy them a haircut if you hear them talking about their service while you're at the barber shop or hair salon.

2. Buy their dinner if you know they served.

3. Buy them a round of beers.

4. Pay for their gas if you see someone in uniform at the gas station.

5. If you are in line at the fast food register, go ahead and pay for the service member behind you, too. Just say, "And whatever he/she wants, put it on my tab." And then tell him or her, "Thanks for your service."

6. You don't have to actually pay for anything. If you see service members or veterans anywhere, just go up to them and briefly say, "Thank you." And then walk away. It will brighten your day, and it will make them feel amazing!

7. Come up with your own way to make a veteran or service member feel good, and post it on my Facebook page at www.Facebook.com/ChrisBedgoodFlippingSanDiego.

Bedgoodisms At-a-Glance

---◆---

Your quick reference to all things Bedgood.

1. **Don't Be Afraid To Fail... Forward**

2. **Motivation: Create Your Own Destiny**

3. **Make Your Own Luck**

4. **The Law Of Exponentiality**

5. **Networking & Face Time**

6. **Measure Your R.O.T.: Return On Time**

7. **Treat Your Daily Life Like A Business**

8. **Perfection Can Be Your Enemy**

9. **Know Your Risk Tolerance**

10. **Finding The Right Mentors**

11. **Being A Pessimistic Optimist Can Be A Good Thing**

12. **Hold Yourself Accountable, No One Else Will**

13. **Learn To Say No**

14. Find People Who Believe In You... And Leave The Others Behind

15. Learn The "Take Away"

16. Find A Way Around The Wall... Any Way

Bonus: Sharing The Wealth Has Made Me Wealthy

So Many People I'd Like to Thank

———— ◆ ————

...and who believed in me along the way

The U.S. Navy and all its aviators and sailors.

The U.S. Armed Forces, Army, Air Force, Marines, and Coast Guard.

Doug Baldridge – Vietnam Army veteran/Retired Navy 1st Class/P-3 Flight Engineer/747 Captain/Family Man. My mentor on how to live life to the fullest, how to enjoy traveling on a shoestring budget at any age, the comfort of listening to Steely Dan with a glass of red wine, and of being a great friend. Love ya' Doug.

Carolyn Kay Bedgood (Arnold) – You were a fantastic Mother and Nurse. Rest in Peace. Love You.

Don Bedgood – Thanks for being so hard on me when I was young, Dad, and thanks for being there for me as I grew up. You are an amazing man. Love you.

Greg Bedgood – My little brother and a great friend. You always keep me grounded. Love you.

Mildred Arnold – Thanks for being the best grandmother anyone could ever have. Love you Granny.

Kristi Stanbery – You believed in me from the day I met you even though I was broke. Thanks for being there for me. Love you.

Bill Cripe – Pilot and Aircraft Mechanic.

Roger Artz – Flight department vice president.

Chief Denney - Friend and Mentor. Mentor and Friend.

Suzen Sarko - Gave me my first real estate agent opportunity in downtown San Diego.

Erik Weichelt - Past president of San Diego Association of Realtors. Thanks Erik.

Mark Marquez - Past president of San Diego Association of Realtors. Thanks Mark.

Erika Deanda - Guided me when I was a newbie real estate agent. Thanks Erika.

Alice Greliak – Realtor Extraordinaire.

Angie Salisbury – Writer/Editor Extraordinaire.

Made in the USA
Lexington, KY
14 October 2016